The Stillness of Winter

The Stillness of Winter

Sacred Blessings of the Season

BARBARA MAHANY

Growing in Life, Serving in Faith

NASHVILLE

THE STILLNESS OF WINTER
SACRED BLESSINGS OF THE SEASON

Copyright © 2020 Abingdon Press

978-1-7910-0755-3

Shutterstock images: Cover image courtesy of Shutterstock/ jamie.sue.photography. Image page 8 and throughout book courtesy of shutterstock/aleksa__ch. Page 10 courtesy of shutterstock/Yuliya Derbisheva VLG. Pages 16, 36, 37 courtesy of shutterstock/crystaaalina. Pages 17,33, 57 courtesy of shutterstock/ wacomka. Pages 32, 34, 169, 184, 192 courtesy of shutterstock/abbilder. Pages 38, 96, 97, 167, 176, 177 courtesy of shutterstock/Maria Stezhko. Pages 40,43, 44 courtesy of shutterstock/nld. Pages 49, 162 courtesy of shutterstock/Hanna Kh. Pages 52, 55 courtesy of shutterstock/Tutti_fiori. Pages 54, 173, 175, courtesy of shutterstock/Yulia She. Page 69 courtesy of shutterstock/Natalia Hubbert. Page 77 courtesy of shutterstock/Anastasia Mazeina. Page 82 courtesy of shutterstock/varvara.sharovatova. Page 109 courtesy of shutterstock/Lemaris. Page 113 courtesy of shutterstock/Prompan Mfish. Page 124 courtesy of shutterstock/Thoom. Page 126 courtesy of shutterstock/PLotulitStocker. Page 137 courtesy of shutterstock/Elena Pimonova. Page 144 courtesy of shutterstock/ Anna Violet. Page 165, 170, 171, 185, courtesy of shutterstock/Maria Stezhko. Page 168 courtesy of shutterstock/Apelsishka_art. Page 179 courtesy of shutterstock/ Mark Atkins. Page 181, 183 courtesy of shutterstock/Yu-lya. Page 181, 183 courtesy of shutterstock/Irina Vaneeva. Page 182 courtesy of shutterstock/vector_ann. Pages 188, 190 , 191 courtesy of shutterstock/ Natalia Hubbert. Page 191 courtesy of shutterstock/first vector trend. Page 205 courtesy of shutterstock/Elena Pimonova. Page 205 courtesy of shutterstock/Daria Ustiugova. Page 207 courtesy of shutterstock/runLenarun. Page 212 courtesy of shutterstock/Galyna Gryshchenko. Page 218 courtesy of shutterstock/Lyubov Tolstova.

Creative Market images: Images page 8, 12, 15, 19, 35, 50, 52, 60, 92, 98, 102, 104, 107, 114, 163, 186, 187, 196, 200 courtesy of Creative Market/ Anastezia Luneva. Pages 20, 21, 23, 208 courtesy of Creative Market/Kaleriiat. Pages 24, 26, 105, 119 courtesy of Creative Market/ Charliez. Page 41 courtesy of Creative Market/Graphic Blue Bird. Pages 45, 47, 48, 51, 53, 57, 93, 95, 101, 115, 120, 130, 134 courtesy of Creative Market/Yuliya Derbisheva. Pages 116, 117 courtesy of Creative Market/Gringoann.

Cover and interior design by Jeff Jansen | Aesthetic Soup

20 21 22 23 24 25 26 27 28 29 – 10 9 8 7 6 5 4 3 2 1
MANUFACTURED IN THE PEOPLE'S REPUBLIC OF CHINA

Contents

In the Stillness of Winter

Winter abounds in wonder. Wonder is the dawn, after a snowfall, when the world is quelled by a quiet like no other quiet. When icy mosaics are etched on the panes of the window. When the red bird of winter—hope perched on a bough—shatters the washed-out tableau. Wonder is the soul burrowing into the darkness, kindling the flame deep within.

At heart, this is a book of wonder. Of beholding the everyday miracle. Of wrapping our arms around the Holy Within and the Holy All Around.

Consider this a field guide to wonder, certainly, and wisdom, perhaps. It borrows, in spirit, from the almanac, the scrapbook, scribbled field notes, assorted jottings, and, on occasion, the banged-up recipe file that's tucked on my kitchen shelf.

It's a book I hope you come to know as something of a friend, a gentle-souled companion you might choose to cozy up with.

It unfurls month by month, drawing deep into the folds and the nooks and the crannies of winter, the season of stillness.

I have long been enchanted, enraptured by the miracle of this holy Earth's turning, its invitation to follow the circle of the year, the depth of winter, quickening of spring, plenitude of summer, autumnal awe. And to discover, back to winter once again, that really it's a spiral; while the world around has echoes of the familiar—from the slant of winter's light, to the particular nip in the air—who we are deep inside is ever ripening, hardly the same one winter to the next.

The aim, at every turn, is to hold the holy hour up to the light. Extract the essence, the marrow, the deep-down glory, the everyday gospel.

Month by month, season upon season, we march through time. We choose: savor—savor it all, every blessed morsel. Or let it slip away, unnoticed, unrecognized for the majesty, the miracle, each moment offers.

Pay close attention, is the beckoning. Behold the Holy Hours.

December

December, month of
the longest night, when
minute by minute our dot
on the globe is darkening.
Yet darkness to me is alluring;
it calls me to turn inside, to
be hushed, to pay attention.

December Field Notes:

In this darkest month, when the solstice marks the sun's lowest point in the year, and night stretches to its longest, ancient peoples feared the solar light might never be kindled again. Back in pagan Scandinavia, Nordic merrymakers lit up Juul logs, slugged back mead, tended fires all night long. Romans got downright riotous, decking halls with rosemary and laurel, burning lamps through the night, carrying on crazily, in hopes of warding off the spirits of darkness. And the Incas went so far as to try to tie the sun to a hitching post, a great stone column, to keep it from escaping altogether. Nowadays, trusting in the dawn, we needn't be afraid. Rather, longest night beckons quietude.

❄ Full Cold Moon, or Long Night Moon, lights the long, long night. Even more so, because with the sun so low across the sky, winter moon arcs higher, and takes longer than during the rest of the year to cross the night sky.

❄ The guiding star in this night sky is not the biblical star of Bethlehem. Rather, Orion, the hunter, and Gemini, the twins, move to center stage as winter begins. And all the darkness brings its own reward: a nighttime canvas stitched in deep-sky splendor. Double and triple stars abound, each a celestial wonder—among the most glorious of the astronomical calendar.

❄ It's not all ice and snow blanketing crust of Earth; rainy season begins in the Pacific Northwest. And woods aren't wholly barren, with sumac and bittersweet berries staying ripe through the winter, ready fuel for the famished. Bald eagles soar in from up north, for milder overwintering. Great Horned Owls pair up and fashion love songs as they do so. Chipmunks go underground for the long winter's nap. But fox and gray squirrel fancy all the roaming room and make the best of it with Mother Nature's call to mate.

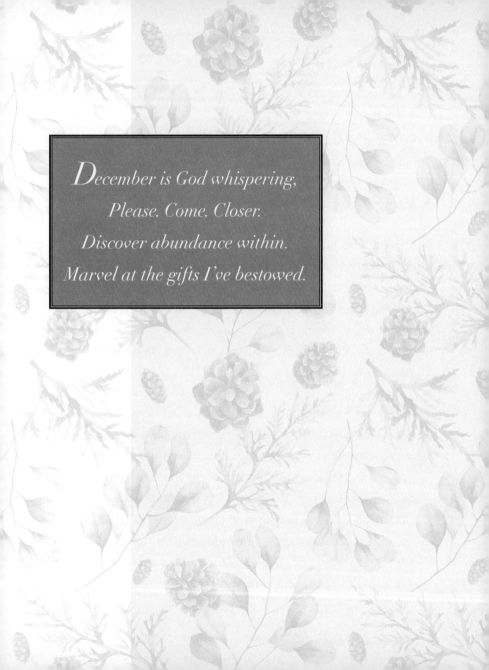

December is God whispering,
Please. Come. Closer.
Discover abundance within.
Marvel at the gifts I've bestowed.

December: Sacred Invitation

There is something about December, all right.

I call it a gift.

It might be my ancient Celtic roots, or maybe it's my monastic inclinations, but give me a gray day, a day shrouded in mist and peekaboo light. Give me a shadowed nook to slip into. And I wrap myself in the cloak of utter contentment.

It's dark all right, come December, month of the longest night, when minute by minute our dot on the globe is darkening.

Yet darkness to me is alluring; it calls me to turn inside, to be hushed, to pay attention.

Mine is a lonely outpost; December, most everyone else complains, is unbroken darkness.

The way I see it, though, maybe the *saddest* thing is, we've blinded ourselves to the darkness. Cut ourselves off from the God-given ebb and

flow of darkness and light. It's poetry, the rise and the fall of incandescence and shadow. But, mostly, it's lost on us.

The truth is: darkness draws out our deep-down depths. Darkness is womb, is seed underground. Darkness is where birthing begins, incubator of unseen stirring, essential and fundamental growing.

The liturgical calendar, prescriptive in its wisdoms, lights the way: it gives us Advent, season of anticipation, of awaiting, of holding our breath for spectacular coming. Season of dappling the darkness with candled crescendo.

And therein is the sacred instruction for the month: make the light be from you. Deep within you.

Seize the month. Reclaim the days. Employ ardent counterculturalism, and do not succumb.

December, I like to think, is when God cloaks the world—or at least the northern half of the globe—in what amounts to a prayer shawl. December's darkness invites us inward, the deepening spiral—paradoxical spiral—we deepen to ascend, we vault from new depths.

At nightfall in December, at that blessed in-between hour, when the last seeds of illumination are scattered, and the stars turn on—all at once as if the caretakers of wonder have flown through the heavens sparking the wicks—we too, huddled in our kitchens or circled round our dining room tables, we strike the match. We kindle the flame. We shatter darkness with all the light we can muster.

Here's a radical thought, for December or otherwise: live sacramentally—yes, always. But most emphatically in the month of December. To be sacramental is to lift even the most ordinary moments into Holiness. Weave the liturgical into the everyday.

December is invitation. December is God whispering, *Please. Come. Closer. Discover abundance within. Marvel at the gifts I've bestowed.* Listen for the pulsing questions within, the ones that beg—finally—to be asked, to be answered. Am I doing what I love? Am I living the life I was so meant to live? Am I savoring or simply slogging along?

December invites us to be our most radiant selves. And we find that radiance deep down in the heart of the darkness. The darkness, our chambered nautilus of prayer. The coiled depths to which we turn in silence, to await the still small voice that whispers the original love song. Chorus and refrain, inscribed by the One Who Breathed the First Breath: make room in your heart this blessed December, make room where the birthing begins.

December's Whisper

The December I am drawn to, the one that most emphatically, insistently, invites me in, is the one that beckons in whisper.

The apex of my counter-culturalism, perhaps, I take my month of longest night in slow sure sips. Timpani belongs to someone else. My December is one that calls for quiet.

Long stretches of hours in which the simmering on the stove, the ticking of the clock, the occasional squawk of the jay at the feeder, those are the preludes, the quarter notes and half notes that I take in.

There will come, I'm certain—because year after year it comes—the one annual carol I play over and over, cranking the dial till the house shakes, and I worry the next-door neighbor might come running to see if all is well.

I've spent the week preparing, whisking away autumnal vestige, ushering in soon-to-come winter. I've stockpiled seed in 20-pound sacks (several, so far), and vats of ice-melting pellets for the dawn when the ice comes. I've piled pumpkins and gourds in the old trough my squirrels and possums (and the occasional uninvited skunk) depend on, the autumn's feast now theirs for winter keeping. I've snipped boxwood and spruce, tucked branches of both into window boxes just below the ledges, where Jack Frost will soon anoint the panes. I've strung Italian star-lights around and through the posts of my picket fence. When the sun drops down, I won't be alone in the dark. There is twinkling at the edge of the yard, front and back. And a candle flickers atop the kitchen table.

It is all a part of the coiling in. The nautilus of deepening prayer.

The prayer that fills me most is the prayer that slowly and silently seeps to the tucked-away places, the ones that await the season of stillness, the places unlocked by the smells and the bells of December: pungent clove, star anise, hissing wick, crackling log, twilight's first star and the night's last ember at dawn.

It won't be long till somehow I crank the oven, haul out the canisters, bang my grandma's old maple rolling pin against the cutting board's edge. My coterie of cookie cutters each play a role in their own sugarplum suite.

One day this week I hauled a turkey carcass from the fridge, and plunked it in my deepest pot, the vessel for soup-making for a dear, dear friend whose newborn is just home from the ICU, and for whom I've cooked up all the sustenance I could imagine: brown rice, pulled-from-the-earth plump knotty carrots and fennel and garlic, savory stock, a handful of parsley.

I'll deliver my brew well before sundown, and in return I'll drink in the newness, the perfection, of a babe just birthed, cradled more tightly and tenderly than ever imagined because ICUs do a mighty fine job of reminding how blessed it is to be finally sent home, untethered from the web of too many tubes and the fright that shakes a new mama and papa—and all those who love them—down to their rickety bones.

(There is, of course, no ailment that the balm of a day-long simmering kettle won't cure; even a newborn mama's terrible tremble is certain to be chased away at the very first shlurp of that omnipotent zoup.)

Indeed, these are my December liturgies, day after day. Intercessions of prayer, punctuated by plain old worldly deadlines. I attend to my errands and chores and assignments—laundry is folded and ferried, empty shelves of the fridge re-stocked, sentences are typed and essays submitted.

But the work that's most heavenly, certainly, is the quiet work of the soul come December. The making way, making room at the inn, in the heart.

The grace of December, the gift of December, is in the quieting, the hush of the sacred whisper. The vespers that hallow—make holy—the heart. Make room in the heart this quiet December.

Smell, aka Simmering Wintry Incense

A rite of winter, a sort of home-spun incense that I call, simply, Smell. It fills the house (or at least the kitchen) with "winter," and the making of it each morning is almost sacramental.

I have an old small red pot and, once the chill of winter rolls in, I take to filling it each morning with spices and orange peel, all doused in water, which I softly simmer through the day—whenever I'm home. My little red "smell" pot holds these ancient spices: star of anise, cinnamon stick, a small handful of cloves, a bay leaf, an orange peel from a bowl of dried peels nearby. The heavenly perfume that rises is one that soothes and stirs and reminds me Christmas is coming, these are the days for simmering stillness, for gathering the gifts of the earth and sending them heavenward. Little puffs of prayer cloud.

It's soul food, indeed. Deep-breathed, fuel for the soul . . .

Should you be inclined to stir up a batch of your very own "Smell": gather 1 whole star anise (from any spice shop); 1 cinnamon stick; a palmful of cloves (let's say 6); 1or 2 bay leaves; the peel of 1 orange or clementine. Plop into a small cookpot. Cover with water. Set to simmering on the stove. Inhale to your heart and soul's content.

Counting the Days

I am practicing Advent. Really practicing. Paying attention. Giving in to the season in ways that wash over me, seep into me, bring me back home to a place I may never have been.

Like a child this year, I have a just-opened sense of these days.

I am, for the very first time, not counting down. Not ticking off days and errands to run like a clock wound too tightly.

Instead, I am counting in a whole other way. I am counting, yes, but the thing that I'm doing is making count each one of the days. I am counting the days in a way that takes time. That takes it and holds it. Savors it. Sucks out the marrow of each blessed hour.

I am this year embracing the darkness. I am kindling lights. I am practicing quiet. I am shutting out noise and filling my house with the sounds of the season that call me.

I am practicing no. *No* is the word that I'm saying to much of the madness. No, I cannot go there. No, I cannot race from one end of town to the other. No, I will not.

I am practicing yes.

Yes, I will wake up early. Will tiptoe alone, and in quiet, to down in the kitchen, and out to the place where the moon shines. Where the early bird hasn't yet risen. But I have. I am alone with the dark and the calm, and I am standing there watching the shadows, the lace of the moon. I am listening for words that fill up my heart. It's a prayer and it comes to me, fills my lungs, as I breathe in cold air, the air of December, December's most blessed breath.

Yes, I am redressing my house. I am tucking pinecones and berries of red, in places that not long ago were spilling with pumpkins and walnuts and acorns.

I am waking up to the notion that to usher the season into my house is to awaken the sacred. It is to shake off the dust of the days just before. To grope for the glimmer amid all the darkness.

December, more than most any month, can go one of two ways.

One trail is all tangled, all covered with bramble. You can get lost, what with all of the noise and all of the bright colored lights.

But December, if you choose, if you allow it, can be the trail through the woods that leads to the light, far off in the distance.

The darkness itself offers the gift. Each day, the darkness comes sooner, comes deeper, comes blacker than ink. It draws us in, into our homes, yes, but more so, into our souls.

It invites us: light a light. Wrap a blanket. Sit by the fire. Stare into the flames, and onto the last dying embers. Consider the coming of Christmas.

I am, in this month of preparing, in this month of a story told time and again, listening anew to the words. I am considering the story of the travelers, the Virgin with Child, the donkey, the man with the tools, the unlikely trio, knocking and knocking at door after door.

I am remembering how, long, long ago, I winced when I heard how no one had room. Open the door, I would shout deep inside. Make room. Make a room.

I didn't know then I could change it. I could take hold of the story; make it be just as it should be.

But I do now. I know now.

I am taking hold of that story, the way that it's told this December. I am, in the dark and the quiet, making the room that I longed for. For the three in the story, yes, but even for me.

I am preparing a room at the inn. The inn, of course, is my heart.

It's the Quietest
Moments that Speak to Me...

The shoes of the boys I love, the shoes I've always filled before dawn on the sixth of December, the Feast of St. Nick, those shoes are hundreds of miles away this dawn. Likely lined up like straight-back soldiers in one's law-school apartment, and in a dorm room half as far away, I'm guessing they're jumbled, strewn under a desk or a bed, or a sweatshirt and socks heaped on the floor.

To grow up in this old house was to wake up to foil-wrapped chocolates and oranges and surely a candy cane stuffed in the wide-open maw of your boot or your slipper or sneakers, a pair that grew by the year (all the more room for more chocolates), and always was left by the bedroom door on the night of the fifth.

I've always made as much of a folderol over this "Little Christmas" as I have over the one that's gotten so noisy.

It's the quiet moments of Christmas, the unexpected kindnesses, the silence on a star-stitched night that stir the holy in me. I enter into the season in whispers. Find myself pulled into tide pools of unspoken wonder. Thrill like a kid with her nose pressed to the windowpane when I find myself face to face with the modern-day version of an elf. If you keep watch, and I'd advise that you do, there are jolly fine elves all around.

This time of year, I do make a list. A list of out-of-the-blue elves and dollops of kindness that have plopped into my lap:

❋ The gas station owner who piled his tools into a cardboard box and drove me the three blocks to where my own car wouldn't start, where he proceeded to ping and tap-tap-tap to try to get the key in the ignition to turn (it would not). He charged not a penny and did the whole thing with a serious smile and multiple insistences that this was not at all out of his way. (On a Sunday morning no less.)

❄ The college roommate from long, long ago who sent me a shoebox bursting with the itty-bittiest gingerbread babies, each one iced and strewn with cinnamon hearts, each one dangling from a skinny red thread she'd taken the time to tie in a loop.

❄ My brother who's driving two hours (each way) to the snow-covered storybook village where our freshman in college is just about to start his first round of finals. The plan (hatched in the spontaneous joy of the moment) is to fetch the kid after his last exam, bring him back to Cleveland for a Friday night's feast and a snooze on an airbed, then tuck him onto a Greyhound bus for the long ride home, where he'll finish his papers in the cozy quiet of home.

My list isn't done; it's just getting started. But I know from years and years of paying attention that those catch-you-by-surprise, take-your-breath-away moments are the ones when the Christmas seeps in.

It's something like watching water whirl down a drain; it's a force you can't stop, it's a pull you can't really see. But you feel it. You know it. The moment sucks you right in, a sinkhole of joy, of wonder, of can-you-believe-such-kindness-exists? And suddenly, deep down inside, you're inside a snow globe of heaven on earth.

Christmas comes in certain spoonfuls, best swallowed all along the way, through the quiet you carve out of the noise. By the time the day itself arrives, you'll have savored its coming already.

Merry Christmas-Is-Coming, St. Nick is among us.

Inscribe your own list of caught-by-surprise Christmas kind-nesses here, the ones that might otherwise go unnoticed, unheralded (and be sure to share with those kind-hearted elves who melted you in the first place) . . .

The Sound of Snow Falling

It is December's gift.

Whole clouds of it fell last night. Started with a flake or two, barely noticed, in the gray of afternoon. By dinnertime, the boughs, the walks, the feeders for the birds, had lost their definition, were taking on a girth that might have made them groan.

Except the world was wordless.

The world, when I slipped on my snow-exploring shoes, zipped up my puffy coat, was so silenced by the spilling from the sky, I could, without straining, make out the sound of snow falling.

It's a sound, quite truly, that makes your ears perk up. And your soul, too.

Unlike the pit-a-pat of rain, it is wholly unexpected. Wind, we know is noisy. Humidity, except for moaning of the ones who find it hard to bear, is not. But that comes as no surprise.

The sound of snow falling, then, is singularly soothing and startling. It is a titillation for the ears, a tickling of the nerves that makes them stand at full attention. A sound not heard so often, certainly not in months and months, it came like water to a thirsty traveler. And I could not get enough.

There is a stillness in the first of every winter's snow that feels to me like coming home. It is in that unrippled place, that place where quiet is complete and whole, that I, and maybe you, feel as if the hand of God is reaching down, is showing me the way through snowy woods.

Sometimes, too, I think I hear the sound of God, putting gentle finger to soft lips, shushing.

Shhhhhhh, I hear God say. *Be still*.

What else, I wonder, could slow a world that can't move fast enough? Who else can keep the cars off the road? The cell phones from incessant baying?

There was not a soul outside last night, not when I was there at least, and I was there for quite a while.

This morning, then, is quiet squared. Not even snow is making sound.

It is December's gift, this early snow. It is just in time to serve its highest purpose. To shush a world in full staccato. To make us perk our ears, to see if, this blessed day, we might hear the song of snow falling.

Winter (or December) Solstice

Once again, darkness blankets the hours. Once again, we've come to longest night—in the Northern Hemisphere. The winter solstice arrives per celestial timekeeper, at the precise moment the North Pole is tilted farthest from the sun, and the shadow cast across the northerly globe is at its longest. In the Southern Hemisphere, of course, it's wholly otherwise, with the South Pole tilted nearest the sun, and southerly daylight at its most protracted. It's all the heavenly concordance of light and shadow. Depending on the crosshairs of your latitude and longitude, the solstice falls on or near December 21.

Maybe, deep inside, it's that we're all still afraid of the dark. Or drawn to it.

Either way, as long as we've been two-legged, upright, and wise enough to wield a light-spitting wand (be it torch or battery-fueled flashlight), we've tiptoed toward the longest night, the winter solstice, with an odd mix of awe and wary eye over the shoulder.

With each minute's darkening, ancient folk (and some of us nowadays, too) feared the sun might never shine again. Be

forever extinguished. A burned-out bulb in the blackest of skies. So, they (and we) churned up the wildest rumpus. All but set the place ablaze. Fired up candles and torches and piles of sticks, lest there be no tomorrow.

Solstice science boils down to plain-angled geometry: it's all about tilt. You might say the North Pole turns its back to the sun. The shadow cast is never longer. Nor, the night.

But the drama doesn't stop there. That's not the end of the story. Once we're plunged to the nadir, when it's dark as dark can be, the light begins to pour again, slowly at first—in increments of mere seconds in the days just after the solstice—and then, with lifesaving (and relative) abundance, minute by minute.

In the end, the longest night breaks, exuberantly, into undeniable daylight.

Is that the whole point of this exercise in diminishment, in darkness? Trust in the dawn. Put your faith in the heavenly proof: Light comes again.

Being Still

Curious thing this December, more than ever, it is the stillness that speaks to me. That I seek. That some days I grope toward as if blind and making my way through the woods on nothing more than the steadiness of my footsteps and the fine-grained whorl of my fingertips rubbing up against the underbrush, telling me I've lost my way.

It is as if the deep dark stillness itself is divining me toward home.

Which, of course, it is. It always is.

Oh, there's noise all right this December. Clanging like a cymbal in my ear, the squawking from the news box, the screeching of the brakes.

But I am—in my best moments—pushing it away.

I take it in in stiff long drinks—the news, the noise, the grave distractions—but then I do odd things: I lift the blinds at night so I can watch the snowflakes tumbling. I wind the clock and listen to its mesmerizing tick and tock. I sit, nose pressed to frosty pane of glass, and watch the scarlet papa cardinal peck at berries on the bough.

I am practicing the art of being still.

Stillness, when you look for it, is never far away, and not too hard to grasp.

I find, though, it takes a dose of concentration. And sometimes a stern reminder; I mumble to myself, "Be still now."

I am dropping to my knees, or curling up in bed with incantations on my lips. They carry me to sleep some nights; what better lullaby?

It is, in fact, the heart, the soul, that are the vessels of pure true stillness: those chambers deep inside us that allow for the holy to unfold. The birthing rooms, perhaps, of our most essential stirrings.

To be at one with all that matters. To begin the pulse-beat there where the quiet settles in and the knowing reigns.

It is, yes, in the stillness that the sacred comes.

The Littlest Manger

I lifted baby Jesus out of his tangle of old, old shredded papers.

Mary, too. And Joseph, who carries a lantern the size of a fat grain of basmati.

For all the commotion it took to get to them—the ladder that unfolds from the attic had to be pulled, which meant all the boxes in the upstairs hall had to be moved, then I needed a tall someone to help haul down the big cardboard box, the one marked "BAM Merry

Christmas," and while I was at it, I noticed the attic needed some shuffling of stuff, which meant that by the time I climbed down the creaky stiff ladder, I was chilled to the bone—for all that preamble, I have to admit my Holy Little Family just might be a bit underwhelming. A bit easy to miss.

It's odd perhaps, that I so deeply needed them hauled from the attic. It's not like they're commanding whole stretches of real estate. Not like the mantle is theirs and theirs only.

As a matter of fact, they are tucked right on the ledge of a birdhouse I ferried home from a farm a few summers ago. Tossed it in the back of a pickup, watched it bounce down a long country road. It's a birdhouse built to look like the church on the top of the hill in that sweet farmer town, and, now, it's the perch for my Holiest Littlest Family.

I was practically hungry for the three tiny folk to get out of the box where I lay them each year when it's time to put away Christmas. I was hungry in that way when your soul is silently growling. Like when your tummy needs soup, only this is your soul, and it needs sustenance too.

That little manger—for something ninety-nine folks out of a hundred might walk right past, not even notice—is, like all symbol in life, packed with a wallop of meaning to me.

It is my whole Christmas distilled. It is the essence of a very long journey. It tells the story of a Christian and a Jew, of a life and a love that was never imagined.

The Christian is one who once saw the hand of God everywhere. Once watched, through spread fingers and tears from a pew in a nunnery chapel, as the face of Jesus up on the Cross changed like a Kodak slide show, all kinds of faces—black and brown, wrinkled and gray, a dozen or so, a true tour of the world, in faces—a miracle that spoke in the most certain words: find God in each and every face.

The Jew in this story is deeply observant, bore his own heartache marrying outside of the tribe. Outside of the lines, he colored his life.

We both did.

The question that's posed, and answered, in that small wood-carved trio is this: how in a home—how in the sacred space you build only on trust and faith in each other's capacity to move beyond what you've known all your lives—how do you weave together the Christmas that means everything with the one that always was cast as a threat to your people, your race, and religion?

I started small. I started on tiptoes.

There is no place in my heart or my home for bombast or noise. Certainly not trickery. I am wrenched, frankly, when I read of interfaith families who use Christmas and Hanukkah as some sorts of weapons, a tug-of-war rope to see whose holiday is left standing, and whose topples over. I did not marry a man I love, did not nosedive out of the safe zone, to whittle away my life playing holiday games.

And so, amid a whole carton of hand-me-down wooden carved angels and shepherds and even a platoon of brass-playing penguins, long ago on our very first Christmas, I moved back the tangle of old paper shreds, and there lay Baby Jesus, a toppled Joseph, and upturned Mary, as well.

I remember catching my breath, gasping, and staring at the sweet little family. I lifted each one in my palm.

I knew then, that very first Christmas, that I had a crèche I could softly, quietly, tuck off to the side. Wouldn't ruffle a feather. Wouldn't stir, not even a mouse.

The fact of the interfaith journey is that—if you are paying attention, if you are listening closely—it can be a long, arid road. You might spend a few years in the desert. You might fall on your knees, night after night, praying one thing: dear God, keep the pilot light lit. Don't let it snuff out.

The fact of the interfaith Christmas is you need to be gentle. Need to listen with very big ears to the layers of history. You need to know that a tree isn't only a tree. A tree, when you grew up Jewish, was one thing that separated you from all of your neighbors. You were proud of that fact. It meant, you believed, that you were the people God chose. It meant, too, you were the people painfully persecuted. By Christians as well as the Nazis. At separate times, in separate ways, but persecuted nonetheless.

Never once have we not gotten a tree. My husband, God bless him, has joyfully carried one home, year after year. Last year, he grabbed the fattest one on the lot. Fraser fir, too, the best that there is in the Christmas tree business.

A crèche, though, I feared, might be pushing a little too far. So I joyfully settled my heart into the littlest one that came in the box.

It's always been my own little Christmas. My devotion was quiet, was whispered, in the deep of the night. Or when everyone else in the house had magically vanished, and I was alone.

It carried me through years of not knowing, of finding my

way through this uncharted forest. For a few years there, for a whole host of reasons, my ironclad knowing had been shaken and shattered. I was left holding little but shards.

Still, Christmas came all those years. And I clung to my Littlest Manger. My manger that didn't get in the way, that no one needed to notice. But held me, rapt.

And then, not long ago, I somehow got to the summit. I realized the power of story, regardless of provable fact.

In the utterly simple, deeply profound truth of the matter, I took in the whole Christmas story for the power of its infinite hold: a babe born in a barn; the unlikely virgin mother; the carpenter guardian; the chorus of barnyard critters; the innkeepers who hadn't a room; the bright shining light in the heavens; the shepherds and journeying kings.

For a minute there I thought maybe I needed to find myself a crèche bigger than the tips of my fingers. Thought, really, it's time to not tiptoe.

But then, I lifted my littlest manger from out of the box. And I realized how perfect it is for the Christmas I believe in with all of my heart: it is Christmas condensed to its delicious, delectable best.

It is Christmas in whispers. It is a babe born in the night. It is a Savior whose very first cry was let out in the straw of a barn. It is the Lord, greeted by shepherds.

And that is a story I am blessed to call mine.

When Wonder Comes for Christmas

When at last the morning comes, I am not unlike the little child at Christmas. Having tossed and turned in anticipation, through all the darkest hours, at first light I throw back the blankets, slide into clogs, slither into a heavy sweater, and tiptoe down the stairs.

For days, I've been stockpiling for my friends. I've corncakes stuffed with cranberries and pinecones wrapped in peanut butter. I've suet balls to dangle from the boughs, and little bags of birdseed, just small enough to stuff in all my pockets. I've a jug of fresh water for all to drink and splash before it turns to winter's ice.

It's time for a Christmas treasure all my own, one I unwrap every year.

My walk of wonder takes me no farther than the patch of earth I call my own, a rather unassuming tangle of hope and dreams and heartache (for what garden doesn't crack a heart, at least once a season?), in my leafy little village.

I carve out this hour of Christmas morn, before the footsteps slap across the floorboards up the stairs, before I crank the stove, and kindle all the Christmas lights.

It's my hour of solitude and near silence, as I tug open the back door and step into the black-blue darkness of the minutes just beyond the dawn.

It's my chance to take in the winter gifts of my rambling, oft-rambunctious garden plots, and all who dwell among them—the birds, the squirrels, and fat-cheeked chipmunks, the old mama possum, and, yes, the stinky skunk who sometimes ambles by and sends us dashing in all directions.

And, best of all, it's my

early Christmas moment to reciprocate the many gifts that all the seasons bring me.

I am nearly humming as I make my Yuletide rounds: I fill the feeders, scatter seed, and stuff an old stone trough with what I call the "critter Christmas cakes."

At this scant hour, the black-velvet dome above is stitched still with silver threads of sparkling light. And limbs of trees, bare naked in December, don't block my upward glance at all that heavens offer.

This is where my prayer begins, as I whisper thanks for all the chirps and song, for flapping wings and little paws that scamper—all of nature's pulse beats that bring endless joy and teach eternal lessons.

As light brightens in the southeast corner of the sky, the architecture of the wintry bower emerges. The black of branches—some gnarled, others not unlike the bristles of an upturned broom—etch sharp against the ever-bluer sky.

Exposed, the silhouette reveals the secrets of the trees—the oak, the maple, and the honey locust that rustles up against my bedroom window.

As I come round a bend, gaze up and all around, I cannot miss the nests not seen till late in autumn, when the trees disrobed and shook off their blazing colors.

In murky morning light, the nests appear as inkblots of black among the lacy boughs. Only in winter do we realize how many dot the arbor. There is the contour of the squirrels' shoddy leaf-upholstered hovel high up in the maple, and, down low in a serviceberry, the robins' tuck-point masterpiece of twigs.

While in robust and leafy times, the trees did not let on, but in winter's stripped-down state there's no hiding the part they play in watching over the nursery, shielding barely feathered broods and not-yet-furry baby squirrels from wind and sleet and pounding rains. Or even too much sun.

This cold morning, all is still. Every nest is empty, every birdhouse hollow once again. Where the winter birds cower, where they huddle, close their eyes and doze, I cannot figure out. Somewhere, even at this illuminating hour, they're tucked away in slumber.

It won't be long till the stirrings come, but for now the only sound is the scritch-scratch of brambles and left-behind leaves as they brush against my legs. I make my way among them, along a bluestone path, past all the shriveled blooms of not-forgotten summer.

The moppy heads of hydrangea, now dried and crisped to brown, are bowed but not surrendered, still clinging, even in the cold. And all that's left of all the roses are persimmon-colored full-to-bursting hips, a final exhortation, punctuation on the winter page.

By the time the Big Dipper fades from the morning sky, that early riser, papa cardinal, ignites the winterscape with his scarlet coat. Soon follows the red-bellied woodpecker, a nuthatch or

two, and, not long after, the choristers of dun-robed sparrows, all a-chatter with Christmas morning news.

I take cover back behind a fir tree, where the crowd at the feeder pays no mind. And where, in winter storms, I find the flocks, too, take shelter, the only branches left that promise shield and a place to hunker down. For anyone who wants to hide—too often it's the hungry hawk—these piney limbs are plenty thick.

Then I get brazen, and toss a handful of peanuts to the bristle-tailed squirrels. These are mere hors d'oeuvres, of course, for that trough now spills with Dickensian plenty—among the larder, bumpy apples no one wanted, and pumpkins plucked from the after-Thanksgiving discount bin.

It is all my way of making real my unending gratitude, of bowing deep and soulfully to Blessed Mama Earth.

Morning Prayer for Christmas

As is my way of keeping Christmas, I will bow my head at the dawn, and I will whisper my litany of prayerfulness. It's the essence of Christmas to me: to weave the strands of petition into a whole and mighty salutation to the God who looks to us to uphold tenderness, mercy, and most of all justice. The God who begs us to keep peace here on this most blessed globe, the one of mountains and majesty, fragile bog and feathered flock. The God who gave us this

gift with the undying hope that we'd hold it close to our hearts, and never let it shatter.

Here is my prayer, or at least the first draft of it:

(The more insistent the prayer, the earlier I seem to rise. And so, this Christmas morning, the heavens are star-stitched still, the edge of the dome is soaked still in inky black. The cardinals haven't yet stirred from wherever it is they sleep.

And yet, my heart is bubbling. My prayers rise up from deep inside. They can't wait to take flight, to be put to the airborne parabola, the one that puts wings to their breath.)

I pray for the mothers who have buried a child, the mothers for whom Christmas will never be whole, will ever be hollow. I pray and pray for peace, just a thread of it, to come to them, to wrap for a moment around their aching heart. I pray for one moment's relief from the stinging emptiness that will not be staunched.

I pray for the children who've lost their mother, two in particular I know and love, and countless others I've read about, countless others who cling to the margins of all the merriment. For children without a mother on Christmas, there is no peace, no everlasting peace.

I pray for the men and the women, cold, hopeless, hungry. I pray for the war-shattered masses, left to die in the rubble, awaiting the words—any words—that tell them the world is listening, has heard their cries, awaiting the word that the world is coming, hope is coming to save them.

I pray for the weary souls I see lying under puffy-layered sleeping bags, on cold hard sidewalks, under viaducts, against the grates at the base of shimmering downtown towers.

I pray for my children. I pray that in their hours of darkness, the light comes. That they see how brilliantly they shimmer in the landscape of my heart and my soul. I pray that someday they understand just how wholly they filled me, how they put purpose to my being alive. That each and every day we try and try again to teach each other: this is how you love.

I pray for all of us who, more often than not of late, feel hollowed. Feel jarred and broken by the hatred spewing all around. I pray for our tender hearts and fragile spirits. I pray that we don't topple. And if we do, I pray for someone strong to come along, to reach out a hand, to whisper hope, and pull us to our feet.

I pray for those who haven't a clue how deeply they teach me each and every day—be it a story on the news, or one passing by in the social media whirl. Or someone I bump into at the grocery store, or riding the train, or shivering in the cold as I shuffle down the sidewalk.

I pray for the ones we've lost this year, the ones whose words rumble through my head, through my heart, each and every day. I pray especially for my friend who wrote these words: "Wake up every morning acknowledging just how much beauty is in your world. Pay attention to it, honor it, and keep your heart and your eyes wide open. You won't regret it," she promised.

I pray for the God who catches the words of this prayer, who catches us all.

More mightily than any prayer I pray of late, I beg Holy God to not abandon us now. To not leave us to our sins and our shattered promises. I promise to love a little bit harder, to live more true to the blessing I was made to be.

And this is the prayer I pray most mightily: I promise to love, God, and I beg You to show us—show me, show every single lost and hungry one of us— the way. The holy, certain way...

Amen.

Blessed Be December

In the Christian liturgical calendar December opens in or almost upon Advent, days of expectant waiting, of kindled light brightening against the blanket of darkness that winter brings. Soon after, Nativity, Holy Birth, Hope and Love cradled in a straw-strewn manger. And so unfolds the stillness in the depths of Christmastime. In the Hebrew calendar, too, the darkness brings the Festival of Light, Hanukkah. One by one, for eight sweet nights, the oil burns, the wicks are lit. We are drawn to quietude, keep cacophony at bay. A year of deepening, of paying attention, of inhaling the Holy brings us to blessed stillness as the Sacred anoints our every hour.

A Count-Your-Blessings Calendar

Fourteen Blessings for December

Here, fourteen blessings to stitch into your winter hours, blueprints for beholding the Holy, practicing the art of paying supreme attention. Some are tied to particular dates, others might be sprinkled throughout the month, for homegrown encounters with the wonder-filled.

Blessing 1: We have watched, for weeks now, the slow undressing of the world beyond the sill. There is no hiding in the depth of winter. We battle back darkness with the kindling of lights, and the stringing of branches with all the glitter we can gather. Look within for truest light.

Blessing 2: Mary Oliver, something of a patron saint of poetry, insisted that our one task under heaven's dome is "learning to be astonished." She called herself a student, first and most, of Ralph Waldo Emerson, who taught her—and us—that "the heart's spiritual awakening" is "the true work of our lives." Today, then, is the day we get to work.

Blessing 3: Be blanketed in the holy lull that is the first snowfall.

Blessing 4: Morning incantations at the cookstove: Stir a pot of oatmeal—bejeweled with dried fruits from the pantry—for yourself and the people you love, still tucked under the covers. Blanket each dreamer—and surely your very own self—in blessings for the day, as you draw the spoon through bubbling porridge.

Blessing 5: "I love the dark hours of my being / for they deepen my senses . . . / From them I've come to know that I have room / for a second life, timeless and wide."—Rainer Maria Rilke, Bohemian-Austrian poet (1875–1926).

Winter Solstice: As the solstice brings on winter, celebrate the darkness. Make a bonfire or simply light candles. Throw a log in the fireplace, listen to the crackle. Tradition has it that fires are sparked on the longest night to help the sun get its job done. Give thought to the life that's birthed out of darkness.

Blessing 7: Spying the brown-paper packages, tied up in red-plaid ribbons, all stacked under the fir tree, put thought to Elizabeth Barrett Browning's certainty: "God's gifts put man's best dreams to shame."

Christmas Day (Dec. 25): On the morn of Nativity, wrap yourself in newborn wonder. Awake before anyone else. Light a candle. Look out the window and quietly count your blessings. Fall on your knees, if so moved.

Boxing Day (Dec. 26): Quiet and dark are invited in, not whisked away, come the season of stillness. Be hushed. Punctuate your afternoon's walk with a trail of birdseed sprinkled from winter-coat pockets. Take supper by the fire—or near a cove of candles. Fuel on simple soup and sturdy bread. Read stories by firelight. Tuck children in their beds, while grown-ups keep vigil deep into the night.

Blessing 10: Survival seed, you might call it. Imbued with animation and sparks of magic, surely. Not a minute after it's been dumped, the yard's aswirl with sound and stirrings. On days of arctic chill, it's the least we can do, to stoke the hearts and bellies of the birds who give flight to the day, who fill the boughs and branches with their scarlet feathers.

Blessing 11: Contemplate the wisdom of essayist Henry David Thoreau, who took up residence in a one-room hermitage deep in the woods of Walden Pond: "If by watching all day and all night I may detect some trace of the Ineffable, then will it not be worth the while to watch?"

Blessing 12: Delight in the winged thespians of winter: Keep watch on the flurry of winter's birds coming in for a landing at the feeder, taking turns, shooshing each other away. Ponder this: "Birds are a miracle because they prove to us there is a finer, simpler state of being which we may strive to attain." —Douglas Coupland, Canadian novelist.

Blessing 13: Revel in the child's joys of deep-freeze winter: Candy canes and marshmallows populating steamy mugs of hot cocoa, the only hope for luring frost-nipped limbs in from out-of-doors. Consider it sweetened invitation to deepened conversation.

New Year's Eve (Dec. 31): "Don't ask what the world needs. Ask yourself what makes you come alive and go out and do that, because what the world needs is people who have come alive."—Howard Thurman, author, theologian, civil rights leader (1899–1981).

The December Kitchen:

Plunged into the longest night, when darkness blankets the hours and the celestial timekeeper tells us winter's solstice is upon us, the kitchen isn't merely a place for distraction; it's downright prescriptive. Crank the flame, steam up the panes of the windows, the ones where each morning Jack Frost leaves icy inscription. While bears retreat to their caves, we humans clang pots and baking pans. We stir. We sift. We make swirls out of buttery frosting. And we fill tins upon tins. Overstock the fridge while we're at it. Tis the season for indulgence of the highest order: extra places squeezed along the table, every chair in the house pulled up to the groaning board. Company's coming. Best of all, the ones you love most.

It's Brisket Weather

Borrowing amply from Truman Capote, who in his delicious and utterly memorizable 1956 treasure, *A Christmas Memory*, tells us of his eccentric sixty-something-year-old cousin who presses her nose to the kitchen window, gauges the Novemberness of the outside tableau, and exclaims, "Oh my, it's fruitcake weather! . . . Fetch our buggy. Help me find my hat."

At our house, I have been known to wake up, sniff the air, and proclaim, "It's brisket weather." Whether autumn or spring, the in-between seasons, or even deepest of winter; it doesn't matter at our house. We invent reasons for brisket—or my boys do, anyway. And so it was the other day, as I trotted off to the butcher who had cleaved and wrapped seven and a half pounds of pure red steer, laced heavily with adipose. As he hoisted the slab from the cooler, he glanced at the name—*Mahany*—scrawled on the whitepaper-wrapped log. Then, impishly, he raised one eyebrow and inquired, "That Jewish?" Well, no, Mister Meat Man. But my husband is, our boys are half-and-half, Jewish and Catholic, and we grab at any excuse for brisket, be it Hanukkah (the Jewish wintertime Festival of Lights) or Pesach (springtime's retelling of the

Exodus story) or whenever a kid wings his way home from college.

One of the curious things about being an Irish Catholic mother in a Jewish-Catholic family is that you have no long lineage of Jewish ancestral recipes you call your own. You have, in fact, something far better: an amalgam of adopted Jewish mothers and the best of their best. I've got Ina's matzo balls; Aunt Joni's tips on storing, freezing, and reheating latkes; Liat's hamantaschen; and Audrey's tzimmes with potato kugel topping, that last one cut from the *Los Angeles Times*, now yellowed, and long ago scribbled with Audrey's thoughts on how to improve it.

Brisket I've got in triplicate, and the one I turn to—time after time, for holidays or homecomings—is the one I now call my own, although it came from a friend's mother, a mother I've met only once, at the side of a pool at a seven-year-old's birthday splash long, long ago, where the meeting was doused liberally in chlorinated pool water. But once or twice or thrice a year, my friend's mama and I, we make brisket together—in that way that a hand-me-down recipe stirs kinship to life. Alone in my kitchen, I listen closely as Mrs. Ellin insists it must be Heinz Chili Sauce and nobody else's. Dare not deviate as she guides me through the rinsing and patting dry of the beef slab.

And then it's into the vault of the oven, where the heat has its way, coaxes surrender of sinew and spice. It never takes long, as my friend's mama has promised, till my kitchen is filled with celestial aroma: all chili sauce, red wine, cloves, and pungent drift of bay leaves.

All the while, we are whispering prayers, Jewish and Catholic, for fork-tender, melt-in-your-mouth, mind-if-I-help-myself-to-more. We'll let you know if our brisket prayers are answered.

Welcome-Home Brisket

When you're about to welcome home your far-flung child, or anyone you love—be it the kindled holidays of darkest December, or any old homecoming any time of the year—and you want the whole kitchen bewitched by the heavenly vapors that rise from a long, slow oven. The preamble to this deliciousness comes a whole day before any company's coming, the moment I pull the binder of family recipes off the shelf. I pore over the recipe that's almost a prayer, one I know nearly by heart after so many years. The brisket—however many pounds of it—idles overnight in the fridge, once its exercise in surrender—from muscled slab to fork-tender succulence—is complete. For hours and hours, it's filled the kitchen, filled the whole house really, with olfactory titillation—that mix of chili sauce and bay leaf, brown sugar, red wine, clove and peppercorn. Long before I sink in my fork, I'm swept up in the magic of every last morsel.

Provenance: Harlene Ellin's mom, whose prescription I follow religiously

Yield: Depends on how hungry you are, but you'd be safe to guess this will feed 6

> 3 pounds first-cut brisket (Such things must we learn; who knew from first-, second-, or even third-cut? Fear not; your butcher knows. As does the friendly meat cutter at any market.)
> 1 cup Heinz Chili Sauce
> ½ cup brown sugar
> ¼ cup dry red wine
> ¼ cup water
> 1 small or medium onion, sliced
> 3 cloves, whole
> 6 black peppercorns, whole
> 3 bay leaves

1. Rinse brisket and pat dry with paper towels. Preheat oven to 325 degrees Fahrenheit. In a small bowl combine chili sauce, brown sugar, wine, and water. Mix well. Pour ¼ of chili sauce mixture into a roasting pan. Place brisket on sauce, fat side up. Place onions, cloves, peppercorns, and bay leaves evenly over brisket.

2. Top with remaining chili sauce mixture.

3. Cover roasting pan tightly. Bake brisket for 50 to 55 minutes per pound, or until meat is fork tender. (Pay attention to the math, friends; it makes for a long, slow roasting. A 3-pound brisket will roast for at least 2 ½ hours.)

4. Remove meat from pan and place it in a container. Remove bay leaves, peppercorns, and cloves from gravy, and put gravy in another container. Refrigerate meat and gravy, separately, for several hours or overnight.

5. To reheat brisket, slice against the grain to desired thickness and place in a covered casserole dish sprayed with cooking-oil spray. Remove and discard any congealed fat from gravy. Pour the gravy over the meat. Cover and reheat in a 375-degree-Fahrenheit oven for 30 minutes or until heated through. (Brisket can be reheated in a microwave.) In a word: mmmm.

Aunt Brooke's Cranberry-Pear Relish

Apt, this dish named *relish*. Must be because you can't help but lick the spoon. You relish it, the relish. Its majesty came to me by way of my Upper East Side sister-in-law, the so-titled Aunt Brooke, who, with four hungry boys, knows her way around the kitchen. She turns out capital-D Delicious, and her stock-in-trade defense, often: "It's a cinch." This time, she was straight-talking. Slice, dump, wait. That's about the whole of it. But what emerges is a pot of garnet-jeweled deliciousness. And at our house, it's now synonymous with all that's best about the almost-winter kitchen. We serve it straight through to Christmastime, long as there's a pear waiting to be sliced, and whole cranberries willing to succumb to the cook-stove's sultry steam bath.

Provenance: This gem, a family heirloom from Aunt Brooke, a baker extraordinaire, who dabbles splendidly in cooking, and who is known to the world as Brooke Kamin Rapaport. She long ago acquired this from her Great-Aunt Eleanor Serinksy.

Yield: Enough to fill a medium-sized serving bowl (I often double the recipe, since more is always wanted)

Three Bosc pears, unripened, unpeeled
One package (12 oz.) whole fresh cranberries
½ cup water
½ cup to ¾ cup granulated sugar

1. The art here is in the pear slicing, so keep the slices slender, allowing the curves to tempt. (We're talking long, lean, vertical slices, stem to bum; not, say, chunky quarters. The sinuous pears here are the show-offs, soon to be garnet-robed. Think: the J. Lo of pears.)

2. Toss into pot with lid.

3. Rinse and dump bag of cranberries atop pears in pot.

4. Add water and sugar. Stir but once, taking care not to ravage the pretty pears.

5. Cover, cook on medium flame or heat.

6. Listen closely. When you hear the pop-pop-pop from beneath the domed lid (about 7 to 10 minutes), turn off heat, and let the magic do its thing.

7. Peek in after 15 to 20 minutes. Behold the garnet-hued heap. Stir gently.

8. Serve at room temperature or tuck into the fridge and allow anywhere from half hour to overnight for thickening to occur.

9. You'll relish it all right. Might be a side dish on a groaning board or atop pound cake with a dollop of vanilla-bean ice cream. You'll lick your lips—the very definition of "to relish."

Prayer with Pots and Pans:
Antidote to December Doldrums

The calendar was cajoling. Winking, taunting. Counting down the days till Christmas. And there I was, slumped in my red-checked armchair, curled like a comma, knees tucked tight to my chin. Diagnosis: December doldrums. No matter how hard I tried, I just could not muster the oomph the holidays demand.

So I did the surest thing I know to beat back the mid-December blues: I cranked the oven. I hauled an armload of oranges from the fridge. Grabbed the canisters of flour and sugar. Soon found myself slamming my grandma's rolling pin against a sack of walnuts (therapy with a mighty bang!). Already, I was starting to feel a little oomph in my kitchen rhumba. I grated. I measured and dumped. I inhaled the sweet scent of orange. Delighted at the garnet bits swimming through the mixing bowl of batter. I was baking my way to Christmas. And on the way, I found my merry heart.

There is something deeply therapeutic about not just baking but baking *en masse*. Making like you're a factory of one. I lined up all my baking pans. Buttered, floured in one long sweep. I found it much less onerous to tick through required steps in quadruplicate, so much more satisfying than one measly loaf at a time. There was some degree of super-power in seeing my butcher-block counter lined in shiny tins, a whole parade of Christmas possibility. I found a magic in the multiples. In not just joy times one, but joy by the dozen.

I made a list of folks I love, and folks I barely know. Folks who might do well to find themselves cradling a still-warm loaf of cranberry-orange-walnut holiday bread. It took hours, of course. Because each batch demanded an hour in my crotchety old oven, the one that deals in approximation rather than precision. The one that might respond to Fahrenheit, or might play in Celsius. It seems to change its mind day by day. All the while I cranked Christmas tunes (truth be told, I played "Mary, Did You Know?" till even my little smartphone called it quits, fritzed from the too-many times I punched "replay").

And therein came the joy. The simple act of drumming up a recipe, ticking off the short list of recipients, wishing more than anything I could wander down the lane to souls I love who live miles or time zones away. Suspended in a day's-long animation, in the act of making plump golden-domed loaves from scoops of this and pinches of that, it was December's holy balm.

This seems to be a season, in this particular whirl around the sun, when old tried-and-true rhythms and routines just aren't working. But scooping your way through a whole sack of flour, grating the zesty peel off a whole orchard of oranges, it held out hope. It nudged me from the dark shadow of ho-hum, into the more glimmering terrain of well-it's-Christmas-after-all. And at every house where I rang the bell, and left behind a loaf, I felt a little thump inside my heart. Every once in a while, someone was home, which led to invitation to step inside, to shatter the cloak of isolation that harbors all of us inside our solitude and day-long silence.

It's a merry tradition, the merriment that's spread by the baker's dozen. The simple act of creation—not just for me or mine, but for folks beyond my own front stoop. The simple equation of making to give away. Addition through subtraction.

Midday I found myself thinking I should take this up for all sorts of holidays, for Groundhog Day, perhaps, for Flag Day. For the annual First Wednesday in September (a holiday I just declared). Point is, sometimes the distance between loneliness and shared company is no farther than the few footsteps from my front door to a door across the way, or down the block. It's no farther than the mailman's empty hands once he drops off my daily pile of circulars and bills.

No farther than the garbage fellow whose heart-melting smile is carrying me through these days.

It's not escaping me this year that, given the chaos that blankets the globe, the deeper I burrow into my shadowy silence, the harder it can be to extricate myself from the depths—and the doldrums.

And sometimes a simple place to begin the cure is with the canisters that line my kitchen corner. And that cranky oven that lives and breathes to warm my kitchen—and, indeed, my soul.

Psst. Here's the recipe (from Gourmet *magazine, via epicurious.com) that got me started. I vamped, as always, from there: more orange zest, more nuts.*

Cranberry-Orange Nut Bread (By the Dozens, Or All by Its Lonesome)

At my house, come middle December, this sweet bread recipe all but bangs on the recipe tin, begging for sudden and urgent release. And with it, the urge to bake assembly-line style. Oh, sure, it stands on its own, but there's something about each golden-domed loaf that makes it more cheery in multiples. *En masse* is the key here. Once you get rolling, lining up tins like so many soldiers, baking in bunches seems to double (or triple) the joy of it all.

Yield: Makes 1 loaf (though I'd heartily recommend doubling or tripling till you've baked for every house on your block)

> 2 cups all-purpose flour
> 1 cup sugar
> 1 ½ teaspoons double-acting baking powder
> 1 teaspoon salt
> ½ teaspoon baking soda
> 1 stick (½ cup) cold unsalted butter, cut into bits
> 1 teaspoon freshly grated orange zest
> ¾ cup fresh orange juice
> 1 large egg
> 1 cup coarsely chopped fresh cranberries
> ⅓ cup coarsely chopped walnuts

1. In a food processor or in a bowl with a pastry blender, blend together flour, sugar, baking powder, salt, baking soda, and butter until the mixture resembles meal and transfer the mixture to a large bowl.

2. In a small bowl whisk together zest, juice, and egg; add to the flour mixture, and stir the batter until just combined.

3. Stir in cranberries and walnuts and transfer the batter to a well-buttered 9-by-5-inch loaf pan.

4. Bake in the middle of a preheated 350-degree-Fahrenheit oven for 1 ¼ hours, or until a tester comes out clean.

5. Let bread cool in the pan for 15 minutes and turn it out onto a rack.

6. Inhale the pure joy of having baked your way to holiday bliss. Wrap each loaf in shiny tin foil, tie with a floppy red grosgrain bow (or silver or gold or Hanukkah blue). Tiptoe into the cold, and commence your delivery. You'll be humming before you get home. And that's a fine December's promise.

Countdown-to-Christmas
Teatime Tuffets

In my storybook imagination, I sit down to afternoon tea with steamy pots of chamomile and platters of delicate cutout Linzer heart tarts, those peekaboo windows of almond-rich cookie, the tops and bottoms cushioned with jam and dusted with confectioner's powdery drifts. But the truth is, I'm not such a precisionist, not in the kitchen anyway; I'm more of a slap-dasher. I live to improvise. A splash of this. A *soupçon* of that. Which isn't what's called for in the baking department. There, where we roll out the well-chilled dough and employ the menagerie of tinware cutters, we need patience. And fine motor skills that escape me.

Which brings me to my Christmas tea nibble of choice: the thumbprint nest. A plump tuffet of buttery dough, rolled in a collar of smashed bits of pecan, impressed with a thump of my thumb, dolloped there in the thumb-well with a spoonful of jammy delectability. Looks to me like a robin's nest in the springtime, a likeness that puts flight to my heart, most especially in the darkening winter. And all that rolling and pressing, it's an excuse to play with your food, disguised as pastry making.

And so, in the teatimes that twirl still in my dreams, and in the countless ones that animated my long-ago days with both of my boys, when a company of stuffed bears plopped down to join us, I opt more often than not for the roll-'em-and-press-'em delight, the raspberry thumbprint. In a pinch, when teatime was beckoned with little notice (and, trust me, this works amid holiday overload), I reached in the pantry (always stocked) for that tried-and-true emergency backup, Pepperidge Farm's Gingerman cookies, adorable crisps that quite nimbly prance across the tea tray. Or nearly as grand as a thumbprint, Walkers Pure Butter Shortbreads, easily dunked in a vat of raspberry jam or preserves (a store-bought move that approximates the thumbprint in taste if not adorableness, and thus has rescued many a tea from the brink of sweets deprivation).

Multiple-Choice Thumbprint Nests

When the civilized art of taking tea entreats, and the cookie platter begs to be heaped with concentric circles of sweets. When not any lump of plebian dough will do, because the occasion is intended to infuse a jolt of joy into even the dreariest day. We're indulging in multiple-choice here because I'm giving you options: A.) stick with old-fashioned jam (I'm keenest on raspberry); or B.) go modern, Nutella, the glorious European chocolate-hazelnut spread; or C.) for true boundary-expansion, a dollop of *dulce de leche* (it's been called "a more worldly caramel," and it comes in a can). And, finally, D.) whichever your choice, you'll not draw one dollop of protest.

Provenance: Jean Paré's Company's Coming: Cookies + Land O'Lakes Butter *back-of-the-box recipe + genius baker Susan Spungen in the* New York Times

Yield: 40 cookies

  1 cup butter, softened
  ½ cup brown sugar, firmly packed
  ½ teaspoon almond extract
  2 eggs, separated
  2 cups whole wheat flour
  1 teaspoon baking powder
  ¼ teaspoon salt
  1 cup chopped pecans
  ½ cup raspberry jam*
      *Thumbprint twist: If your sugarplum visions tend

more toward the chocolatey-hazelnut or *dulce de leche*, and less so the jampot, swap out the jam and pecans, and bring on the trio below:

⅓ cup Nutella (ditto *dulce de leche*, should that be your thumbprint of choice)

½ cup chopped hazelnuts (stick with pecans, if you're doing the *dulce*)

flaky sea salt

1. Preheat oven to 325 degrees Fahrenheit.

2. Cream butter and brown sugar; add almond extract; beat in egg yolks.

3. In separate bowl, combine flour, baking powder, and salt; add to butter mixture and mix well.

4. Form dough into 1-inch balls; dip in egg whites to coat; roll in chopped pecans (or hazelnuts, if you're going for the Nutella twist); place on ungreased baking sheet 2 inches apart.

5. Here comes the fun part: press your thumb into the middle of each ball of dough, making an indent and creating your own little nest shape.

6. Bake for 5 minutes.

7. Remove from oven and quickly press the indents again with your thumb; return to oven and continue baking for 10-15 minutes.

(Keep close watch; once the edges begin to golden, you'll want to grab your oven mitts and rescue the nests.)

8. Remove from the oven and fill indents with jam (or ½ teaspoon Nutella or *dulce de leche* per nest, plus a sprinkle of flaky sea salt) while cookies are still warm.

9. Cool completely. Tuck in cookie tin (with lid) lined with wax paper for safekeeping, up to three days. Or perch atop your favorite cake pedestal and ferry to the tea table. It won't be long until there's nothing but crumbs and the vivid memory of Christmasy tea for two (or more) hearts.

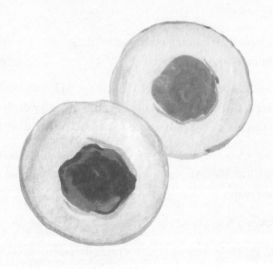

A Christmas Gift . . .
Christmas Eve Elves' French Toast

It's been tradition, long as I can remember, that, come Christmas morn, I'm first one out from under the bedsheets. I've been known to take two steps at a leap, to plug in the tree, and get to work in the kitchen. For years, that meant Christmasy coffeecake, à la page 337 of the highly-splattered *Silver Palate Good Times Cookbook*.

But then I enlisted the Christmas Eve elves. In short, their magic trick is this: overnight soak, swift slide in the oven, and—poof!—rising cloud of cinnamon, yolk, and butter. Suddenly, I discovered more time for sitting alone under the tree. And, with far less fuss, the vapors seeping from the oven smelled just as get-out-of-bed as that yeasty rise, on a morning when eager boys need little stirring to spring from under the covers. It's pure prestidigitation, too, on any snowy morn, when those who snooze in your beds need an extra dollop of oomph to arise and seize the day.

Provenance: Inspired by a long-ago recipe in the Chicago Tribune, *though my own fiddling at the cookstove might make this unrecognizable from the original.*

Yield: One 9-by-13 casserole

1 loaf challah (the braided egg bread, or whatever holiday loaf strikes your fancy), cut into eight 1-inch-thick slices, or however many snugly fit your 9-by-13 baking dish

2 cups whole milk

1 cup cream (it's Christmas, after all)

8 large eggs

4 teaspoons sugar

1 tablespoon best vanilla extract

Few shakes cinnamon

1 orange, grated (if you're so inspired)

¾ teaspoon salt

½ cup dried fruits (the jeweled bits of garnet cranberries, plump apricots, make the bake dressed-up enough for Christmas)

2 tablespoons butter, cut into small pieces

Powdered sugar, for dusting

Maple syrup, honey, or your best Christmasy jam

1. Generously butter 9-by-13-inch baking dish.

2. Layer bread slices across bottom of dish so it's completely covered and filled to the top.

3. In separate bowl, mix milk, cream, eggs, sugar, vanilla, cinnamon, orange rind, and salt.

4. Pour over bread. Toss in a handful of dried fruits, tucking in between and under bread slices.

5. Cover with foil.

6. Refrigerate, covered, overnight. (This is where the Christmas-Eve elves come in.)

7. Next morning, preheat oven to 350 degrees Fahrenheit.

8. Remove egg-cream-bread heavenliness from refrigerator and uncover; it's not necessary to bring casserole to room temperature. Dot the top with butter.

9. Bake uncovered, until puffed and golden, 45 to 50 minutes.

10. Let stand 5 minutes before serving.

11. Dust with powdered sugar, and serve with maple syrup, honey, jam, or whatever sweet stokes your sugarplum dreams. Merry, merry, but of course . . .

Winter's Wonderlist

December

kindling candlewicks, flame-by-flame, ancient armament against the inky darkness . . .

traipsing to the woods, hauling home the sacrificial fir to be adorned in paper chains and tinsel, and a lifetime's accumulation of hand-me-down treasures . . .

curling into the couch, under the red buffalo-check blanket, with O. Henry's "The Gift of the Magi," the Christmas classic that forever defines the art of selfless giving . . .

brown-paper packages tied up with red-plaid ribbons . . .

tiptoeing into the dawn to deliver, by Radio Flyer sled, holiday loaves and love notes to all the neighbors' back stoops . . .

making room on the mantle for baby Jesus . . .

scribble your own here:

January

Year after year, I regard
the first crystalline hours
as new-born, sometimes
so hushed you can hear
the inrush of breath,
sometimes squalling.

January Field Notes:

Full Wolf Moon, sometimes called Old Moon or Moon after Yule, shines down on a sliver of January's days. Back when Native Americans were pinning names to each month's brightest lunar light, wolf packs howled hungrily outside the villages, amid the new year's frigid cold and snow. Orion, the great hunter, rules the night sky. Sunlight, in these nascent weeks just after the longest night, grows by the day, minute upon minute added to the dawn and the twilight.

❄ Deep beneath the earth, bulbs slumber but stirring begins as the scape (or stalk) stretches, and stores of sustenance undergird resurrection, come longer, deeper daylight.

* Cardinals, the scarlet-feathered flock, are first ones to the feeder shortly after daybreak, and last ones headed to the nest at nightfall.

* Off in the woods, Great Horned Owls carry on the timeless rites of wingspread coupling, a not-so-delicate strigine dance two-stepped at the delicate end of the bough. This depth-of-winter month happens to be the peak of Great Horned dalliance. If you put your ear to the wind, you just might hear the Great Horneds' storybook "hoo-hoo-hoooo." While owls romp, black bear cubs are birthed, deep in winter's cave. And the white-tailed deer bucks shed their antlers. New beginnings abound.

I scribble my list of promises.
The ways I hope to be kind.
To be gentle. To forgive.
To try and try again.

January: Blessings, Newborn

January, rising out of the deepest darkness, is at once the tenderest time, and the fiercest—maybe even the bravest. (Do we dare plunge in again? Do we dare pick ourselves up, brush off our knees, and try yet again to be just a little bit more of who God blessed us to be?) Year after year, I regard the first crystalline hours as new-born, sometimes so hushed you can hear the inrush of breath, sometimes squalling. I've been known to curl in an armchair, pick up a pen, and inscribe a letter to the new-coming year. A promise. A hope. An all-shutters-open confession. It goes something like this:

Dear Year Soon-to-Crown,

As I've done before in birthing rooms I will reach out to cradle you, take you in my hands, pull you close against my chest. You'll hear my heart beating, quietly.

I will study you, be in awe of your sudden appearance, your entrance, your being here. There was no guarantee you and I would meet, and therein is the miracle, the often-taken-for-granted miracle. Yet, unmistakably, a miracle. In every way.

Both miracle and blessing, each new year demands my full and unwavering attention. Demands the full attention of all of us standing here on the cusp, filling our hearts and our imaginations with promises, vows, hopes, resolutions of the deepest kind.

I beg you, nascent year, to be gentle. I realize the gentle needs to come from deep inside me. I need to find the holy balm to steady me through rough waters to come. I'm bracing myself with double doses of those few things that have proven to be my salvation: prayer; silence; rampant and unheralded kindness; the rapt company of a rare few companions, deep in the act of holding up each other's hearts.

I will usher you in with all the majesty a new year deserves; I'm quieting already. I'm taking walks in the woods, standing in awe of the crimson flash of the flicker darting from oak to oak.

I'm assuming a prayerful pose under the star-stitched dome of the heavens. I awake with the dawn, press my nose to the window, often step outside, watch the tourmaline streaks stain the eastern edge of night, rise up, rinse the morning sky in diffuse and certain light.

I scribble my list of promises. The ways I hope to be kind. To be gentle. To forgive. To try and try again.

The dawn of each year draws me into my natural monastic state. I would have been such a cheerful monk, walking the moonlit halls, bare feet slapping the great stone slabs, guided by flickering candle's flame. I would have relished a bowl of bean soup simmered all New Year's Eve Day. Would have sliced a thick batonof wheatberry bread. Alas, I'm without monastery walls at this moment in my life, and thus must do without the stone-slabbed corridors. But I've beans and bread and bees' wax. I've a heart awaiting the new year, and all the prayers it will stir.

Be gentle, new year. Be kind. And most of all, be blessed.

Prayer Beads for a New Year

Tucked under the covers with a thermometer poking out of your spout is no way to start the new year. But so it is. And so I type from horizontal perspective. And so this new chunk of time has only one direction to go from here: up.

As I lie and watch out the window, catching a flash of scarlet here, the squawk of blue jays there, I ponder one or two of those lists we're supposed to make this time of year. I can't quite enumerate the things I hope and pray for. After all these years, I've boiled it all down to one more or less all-purpose petition: dear God, make me live and breathe your gentle radiant love. Let me swallow the urge to be unkind. To rebuff the sharp elbow. To turn the other way when insult's hurled my way. Let me practice the Zen of road kindness, refusing to blow the horn, to cut in front, not wait my turn. Let me search for and offer the benefit of the doubt. Let me try harder not to roll my eyes. (Let us institute an apologia for hurling stink bombs at the telly when idiots blather on, and on, and on . . . .) Let me stop the rumor here and now. Not partake of gossip in any way, shape, or form (no matter how juicy).

These are the sins of the everyday. The little molehills that make for mountains, for a continent-wide topography of pain, of bitterness, the sharp and invisible line dividing "us" from "them," that makes enemies of those whose stories we never stop to listen to.

Let us traffic in tiny knots of kindness. Exercise empathy. Imagine how it feels to hurt so much, to be pushed aside, to be left alone on the side of the playground and never find a friend. Imagine never letting go of that hurt.

Imagine what would happen if one morning you woke up and found yourself inside a life where self-absorbed ego had utterly vanished, where extreme and all-consuming navel-gazing screeched to a halt. Where we looked beyond the borders of our own thin skin. Where someone noticed the glimmer in your eye had dimmed. Imagine if someone quietly inquired: are you all right? Did someone hurt you? Imagine a world where we listened instead of trying to talk over each other. Imagine if the ones who take up all the oxygen in the room realized there are others with thoughts to offer. Imagine those rare few souls who live to scatter sunshine, who make us laugh till our bellies ache. Imagine the miracle of the ones who always think two steps ahead, anticipate our hurt, offer tender loving comfort without folderol or trumpet.

Imagine the quietude of saints who walk among us.

Practice, practice, practice.

Forgive yourself on the days when your brokenness shows. Forgive your stumbles. Say "I'm sorry." Say it to yourself.

And just as emphatically, consider a litany of be's: be curious. Be imaginative. Be not afraid to dabble in whimsy. Be willing to put yourself out there. Be humble, so humble. Carve out time each and every day to plug into the immense wonder of the heavens and the earth. Traipse a meadow, a prairie, sandy dunes. Follow a trail into the woods. Count the stars. Realize how small you are against the infinite canvas of the sky. Seek wisdom not simply from picture shows or airwaves, but in the pages of texts—ancient and otherwise—pulled from bookshelves. Deep-dive inside a poem. Make a friend in an unlikely place. Reach beyond your borders.

Make peace.

These are the prayer beads I carry into this new year; these are the petitions I press against my heart.

This is how I walk into this new year. Once I get up and out from under the blankets and the Nyquil.

What petitions might you bring to this new year?

Fresh Start

By accident of birth, I came onto the planet on the third day of a new year, and so all my life—and especially of late—I dwell in my own personal calendar of time delay. The beauty of this stalled beginning is that I've extra hours to contemplate the fresh start. To consider hard and deep just how I might aim to live this year.

I am fueled by aims—a walking, talking, I'll-do-better machine.

And on this gray morning, this morning laced in shadow, my humble vows begin with the quotidian: my shortlist bull's-eyes my knack for piddling away my appointed hours. I'm tackling the humdrum here before I take on the herculean, the stuff that truly might amount to wholesale revolution of the soul.

Once upon a time, one of my persistent stumblings was the way—morning after morning, bedtime after bedtime—I rushed my little ones, always chiming, *We're late, we're late*. I wonder now if that's a soundtrack they'll never forget. I wonder, now that they're gone from my everyday, why I was stuck in a perpetual hurry. Next, and to this very day, I count the home-spun fears that keep me locked inside my comfort zone, too full of cockamamie worries to tread beyond my self-conscribed borders. And, third, the certain shyness that stops me from broadly spreading my wings.

These would be among the litany of my daily sins. Yet, there's consolation, and it comes with a knowing that offers deliverance:

Deep in the truth of all of us lies the rough draft that demands edit after edit.

And so we are blessed, those of us who keep time, who trace the day, the week, the year in spiral.

It is, at heart, a geometry of promise, hope, and, most of all, ascension. It offers us the chance, over and over, to come back to that sacred moment when we stand at the crest of the hill, cast arms wide, salute the heavens, shake off dirt and dust, remap our route, and see if this time round we might inch higher toward the summit.

I don't know a world religion that doesn't devote a chapter, at least, to absolution, cleansing, rinsing. It is as if we are hard-wired for holy resurrection. To rise from our brokenness. To seek forgiveness for our sins and shortcomings. To come back to the fresh start, the blank slate, to try and try again. To believe in the almighty "take two."

And so it is that I come on bended knee. I stand here praying, hoping, promising that my next go-around on this old globe might be one that draws me closer to the unfettered essence I was meant to be. The one not weighted down with doubt and double-guessing. The one that drinks in all the holy waters all around me.

It is, I hope and pray and believe, by little and by little—by little dose of courage, by little kindness, by little gentleness—that we inhale the promise: to shake off our wobbles, stand tall, and launch the climb again.

Epiphany's Eve:
The Midnight Murmurings

Legends enchant me. Stories passed from generation to generation. Stories passed from village to village, hearth to hearth. Legends are the stuff of story and wisdom. One-part enticement and charm, along with a dollop of take-away.

And so, I found myself enchanted when I tumbled upon a legend I'd not heard before. It popped from the pages of *Strega Nona's Gift*, a storybook my faraway forever best friend mailed me for my January birthday.

As I learned while turning the pages, the month of December is one filled with feasts, all of which insist on stirrings in the kitchen. It begins with St. Nick (Dec. 6), flows to Santa Lucia (Dec. 13), then it's Christmas Eve's Feast of the Seven Fishes (Dec. 24), followed swiftly by the midnight feast of Christmas (Dec. 25), and New Year's Eve's Feast of San Silvestro (Dec. 31) when red underwear, for unknown reasons, is required (note to self: go shopping).

It seems the Italians do not stop: they roll the feasting straight into January, which is where this story picks up. According to Strega Nona, my new guide to January feasting, the eve of *Epifiana*—that's Epiphany in Italian, and it comes from the Greek, "to appear"—once again finds everyone cooking. But this time it's for the beasts and the birds, the wee scamperers and the lumbering furry fellows.

"There was a legend that at midnight on the Eve of Epiphany all the animals could speak to each other. It was because the ox and the donkey kept the baby Jesus warm with their breath in the manger. So, the villagers wanted to give their animals a feast . . ."

And that's all the prompt I needed. (Although if you read along in Tomie dePaola's pages, you find that the villagers' motivation is merely to squelch the chance of midnight gossip among the animals, lest anyone's pegged as a stingy old cheapskate who feeds them not. Which I'd say squeezes *some* of the charm out of the equation.)

For years now, my annual feast for the birds is a ritual of the longest night, the winter solstice. I make suet cakes, string cranberries, heap a mound of seed into the feeders. As darkness blankets the hours, I make certain my flocks are fed, and fed amply.

So now I've another excuse. And in honor of the ox and the donkey who bowed down, who warmed the newborn babe with their breath (as exquisite a furnace as I've ever imagined), I baked more cakes, melted more suet, stirred in plump raisins and nuts and seeds. I tossed with abandon on the eve of Epiphany. I filled the old bird bath that now serves as my trough. Scattered cakes and crumbs near the French doors, so I could peek at the merriment come morning.

And sure enough. Not long after dawn, as I wandered out to refill the terra cotta saucer that serves as my birds' winter bath, there before me was one big fat mama raccoon, holding a cake in both of her nimble long-fingered fists.

She glanced up but didn't flinch. She seemed not to mind that I was trespassing quite near to her breakfast. Nor that I was offering a warm drink besides. (Alas, she didn't mutter a single word, nothing close to a *thanks for the chow*; so much for the midnight murmurings. Although she might insist I'd missed the animal chatter by a good six hours.)

And now I've a new excuse for spoiling my herds and my flocks (I like to think of them in masses, as it makes me feel like the shepherd I long to be). There is something deeply comforting in imagining that I'm the guardian of my critters, in hoping they can depend on me to keep their bellies full.

It's a simple notion indeed. But it charms me to no end, and satisfies the tug to be God's caretaker of all creatures, great and small and in-between. In a world that sometimes leaves me gasping for breath, making a feast for my wild things is balm. Especially on a morning when it's 15 below. And the 'coon at my door comes knocking.

One last legend, in short form: the Italians also celebrate Epiphany with the story of Befana, a soot-splattered old woman, sometimes called "the Christmas witch." In the version I love best, a few days before baby Jesus was born, the wise men stopped to ask Befana for directions to the manger where Mary and Joseph and the newborn babe would be found. She hadn't a clue but offered the travelers a room for the night. Come morning, the trio invited her to come along, to meet the Christ child. She declined, saying she had too much housework (therein lies the learning that one oughtn't be waylaid by mopping; you never know what you'll miss). Once the kings had gone on their way, the old lady had a change of heart. Covered in soot, cloaked in a deep-black shawl, carrying her broomstick, she set out in search of baby Jesus. To this day, the story goes, she's still searching. And as she travels from house to house, on Epiphany, she leaves behind fruits and sweets for the good children, and coal, onions, and garlic for the ones who are naughty.

Merry blessed Epiphany....

Epiphany:
Follow the Heavenly Light

Look to the heavens, comes the instruction. Find your way—through the darkness, the murk, the innumerable forks in the road—by seeking the light, divine light. Look to the night star, pooling its radiance onto your path, your uncharted, unmapped, indiscernible path. The one you dare to follow, footfall after footfall—sometimes tremulous, sometimes headstrong, sometimes face to the wind—the whole long journey.

Again, the liturgical calendar—that template for time, but more so for soulful attention—prescribes its wisdom: Christmas, in all its glory, is meant for more than one day. Christmas unspools for twelve days; Quiet Christmas, I call it, the stillness that follows the folderol. Epiphany, then, is the exclamation point, the coda of Christmas, the last of the Twelve Blessed Days. And on the twelfth day of Christmas—the sixth day of the new year—we pause to look up, to study the night sky, scan the clusters of starlight. But also, emphatically, we must look within.

The wonder of Epiphany (*epiphaneia* in Greek, meaning "manifestation" or "appearing"), the whole point laced into the story of the magi, ancient travelers setting out across foreign landscape for destination unknown, is that here, at the dawn of the year, is a feast day positioned to point us in certain direction.

We are all travelers with journeys to take, and miles and miles to go. (Scholars, by the way, count as many as ten wise men, likely astronomers, a numerical revelation that upends the lyrics of many a Christmasy carol, especially that trio who, for the last century and a half, since "We Three Kings" was written, has dutifully followed that yonder star, O star of wonder, star of night.)

The point is, it matters not whether we know how to get where we're going, or where exactly we're headed. What matters is simply the courage to take the first step. And the next, and the next.

And we, too, need illumination, the ancient light of a heavenly star. We need the barest tracing of the path to show us the way. Jan Richardson, a brilliant artist, writer, and Methodist minister, penned an epiphany blessing, titled "For Those Who Have Far to Travel." It begins: "If you could see / the journey whole / you might never / undertake it; / might never dare / the first step / that propels you / from the place / you have known / toward the place / you know not."

Before we get there, there will be gifts, luminous gifts. Maybe not gold, or frankincense, or myrrh.

All along the way, the gift is the epiphany itself, the eye-opening, heart-freeing beholding, the manifestation, yes, of wonder and beauty and mystery. Renaissance scholar and poet Kimberly Johnson says, "I want to live my life in epiphany." So do I. Maybe, so do you.

An ancient Epiphanic practice, one nearly lost in the cob-webbed pages of history, is the blessing and chalking of the house, a rite meant to place God at the entrance to your home, and to protect all who dwell there. It begins with the reciting of a blessing on the house and those who call it home. Then the door is sprinkled with holy water. And, finally, a piece of chalk is blessed, the chalk that will be used to write on the lintel of the doorway the current year plus the first initials of the three wise men: Caspar, Melchior, and Balthasar, written 20 + C + M + B + the last two digits of the year. It is also thought that the wise men's initials—C.M.B.—are an abbreviation for the Latin blessing, "Christus mansionem benedicat" ("Christ bless this house").

Inviting In the Sacred

Someone asked me not so long ago why I search so often for the sacred in my every day.

It's not so much the searching, really, it's that I often seem to stumble on it. Or maybe it exerts a pull, and I can't steer away.

It's just there.

I've found it, often, tucking little ones to bed. Or sitting side by side on stools carved by my brother, in that after-school ebb and flow, when the third-grade day came rushing out in

breathless narrative, and,
every paragraph or so, in
went a bite of apple,
or cookie, or glug of
chocolate milk.

I do, yes, find the
sacred nearly every time
I tiptoe out the door. Not the times
when I'm near a gallop, racing to the station wagon,
keys clunking from my fist, late—too often—for where
I was supposed to be a good ten minutes ago. But in the tiptoe
times, when every pore of me is wide awake and at attention,
when I'm in slow gear, trying not to barrel through, disturb the
peace. Then it's almost certain that the sacred will alight on me,
as a monarch to a black-eyed Susan.

I find the Holy Breath in birdsong, absolutely. And in the
streams of light pouring through the pines, or the crack in the
fence that runs along my cottage garden.

I find knee-dropping humility when I spy the moon. Or when,
weeks behind schedule, a vine I thought had died breaks out in
bloom, a resurrection lesson every time.

I find God whenever I'm alone. Or maybe that's the time
when, at last, I feel the rustling by my side, at my elbow, where my
heart goes thump. Maybe that's when at last it's quiet enough,
still enough, for me to hear the Holy Whispers.

Teaching to See

The lesson: how to regard. How to watch. How to take in the world.

Here's how it unfolded, one morning long, long ago: I bounded the stairs, breathless—and ten minutes late—to roust my little one from his sheets.

He rolled out of bed the way he usually did: somersault off the pillow to sprawled on his back at the end of the mattress, head dangling, flopping like some sort of upside-down rag doll, not too far from the ground. A perfect inverted perch, he decided, for keeping watch out the window.

That's when he announced, "Papa is out on the roof. He's hopping around. I think maybe he's looking for breakfast."

Papa is the red bird, papa cardinal, a character around here who goes by only one name.

After broadcasting every breath Papa was taking out there on the roof, just below the window through which he was watching, my little one reached for the ledge, grabbed the binoculars.

Suddenly, the boy hanging there with his curls topsy-turvy wanted to learn how to look through the little glass circles that, through the wizardry of optics alone, bring the world as close as the end of your nose.

As I tried—it's clumsier than you might imagine— to line up the eye pieces, tried to narrow then widen the space between so they fit to his face, as he attempted to make the looking all clear, not blurry, not too close, not too far, not staring down at the gutter, but trying to get that old bird in his lens, I realized, really, I was teaching the boy how to see.

How to regard. How to watch. How to take in the world without any words.

How to notice the pinhole there on the side of Papa's small beak. How to study the feathers he fluffs when it's cold. How to see the ballet of flurries and ice on the boughs as they shudder there in the deep winter's wind.

He was, for a while, finding it hard. The bird was nowhere in sight. All he saw were the nail heads there on the shingles. Not quite the subject of choice for "Intro to Looking," a beginner's class in the fine art of things to do with your eyes.

Ah, but once he got Papa there in the crosshairs, he didn't move. Didn't flinch. Just froze like a boy with a bird in the palm of his hand. Which, almost, he was.

He might still be there now, only the clock nudged us on, the clock and the notion that school had a bell that soon would be ringing.

But, like clockwork, each morning thereafter, he somersaulted off the end of the bed, grabbed the looking lens from there on the ledge, and began again to scan the sky, and the trees, and whoever decided to land on the roof.

He even tried it at night. Though it's a little bit hard to make out a star with a mere binocular lens. I explained that's where the telescope comes to the rescue, but that would be the next class in the series, and we were only just fumbling with this.

I couldn't have been more tickled that he'd taken so deep a fancy to a sense that can take him so far, a sense that will bring more wisdom and glory than he or I or any of us, really, can ever imagine.

To see is to know, is to understand, is to absorb.

To see is to take in—from the thinnest strand of a spider's web laden with dew to the last dying ember of a star as it streaks through the cosmos—the whole of God's breath.

And it is not every day that any one of us gets a chance to instruct in using the eyes for all that they're meant to take in: The way someone fidgets a spoon while making a point at the table. The color of sky as the last beams of the day paint a pink you'll never forget. The glint of the moonlight on a pine branch heavy with snow. The gleam in the eye of someone you love.

And, oh, what of the things we can't teach, the ones we only can pray they learn on their own: How not to miss the twinge of the hurt deep in the heart; the sparkle of love blooming; the look of intent, of paying attention; how to notice a soul draining toward empty.

Really, so much of it is only just seeing by feeling. It's not unlike Braille, after all. So much of the seeing that matters. It comes through the gift of the eyes, but also by touch and the skip of the heart.

Alas, in those mornings of teaching to see, I realized I was bound, I was tethered to only the lens bobbing there on the end of the cord that slipped over his head.

The rest of the teaching to see I'd teach without lenses. And I will teach, day after day, for as long as I'm here. Over and over, I teach my children to look and look closely.

I teach them the glory of God is there through the lens. But they must open their hearts, as well as their eyes, to soak in the sights. To regard. To watch. To take in the world.

It is the often unnoticed to which I must teach them to pay the closest attention.

I, Too, Have a Dream

There's a grainy audiotape that loops in my head. Always does this time of year. It's the Reverend Dr. Martin Luther King Jr. launching into his "I Have a Dream" speech, from the steps of the Lincoln Memorial in Washington, D.C., back in 1963.

We have come to this hallowed spot. . . .

Every year, come the middle of January, when we pause to consider the modern-day saint and pacifist preacher, I hear the words rumbling, rise to crescendo. Goosebumps prickle down my arms and my spine.

Now is the time to rise from the dark and desolate valley. . . .

Makes me think we must all be bold—especially when it comes to dreams.

We will not be satisfied until "justice rolls down like waters and righteousness like a mighty stream."

I have a dream, booms the voice I hear in my head.

I, too, have a dream.

A long, long time ago I had a real live, wide-awake dream, the sort of dream that shapes a lifetime.

My dream was in the upstairs chapel of a nunnery, far away. Out where hills rolled and corn reached toward the sky. I was only there for the weekend, for what's called a silent retreat. Which means I ate, drank, walked, and prayed in utter, total wordlessness. At least no words that you could hear. There were plenty stirring inside.

It was a Friday night, and I had eaten in silence, tucked my pj's beneath the hard slab that was serving as my bed. I tiptoed up to the chapel and there I knelt. Maybe it was all the silence, or maybe it was something else.

But as I knelt and prayed, staring at the Crucifix, staring at the long muscled legs of Jesus on the Cross, fixing on the nail holes in his palms, taking in the beautiful sorrow, and the peacefulness on his handsome Jewish face, I saw the start of what turned out to be an endless Kodak slide show of faces, one changing into another. I saw old faces, white faces, black faces, brown faces, sallow faces, children's faces. I saw a Native

American, I saw an Asian man, an old one. I saw wrinkles, I saw softness. I saw eyes and eyes and eyes. I was, of course, wiping tears from my own eyes and cheeks and chin. I can't imagine seeing such a sight and not being wholly, deeply moved. The tears, the transcendence deep inside, it's what comes when you feel, sometimes, as if a hand from heaven has just reached down and tapped you, unyieldingly, on the heart.

I knelt. I squeezed my eyes, then slowly peeked them open, to see if maybe this was all a trick that would blink away as fast as it had come. I turned, looked back, and still the faces changed.

I got the message pure and wholly: look for—*find*—the face of God in everyone you meet.

The clincher to this dreamy story unfolded the next afternoon, when I returned, took a seat—near the back, I assure you—in the bigger downstairs chapel. Bravely—through spread fingers—shyly—just a little bit afraid, you might imagine—I raised my eyes again to the face of Jesus on the Cross.

At first, nothing. But then, as I softly sank into prayer, I saw a smile wash across the face of Jesus. It was all the holiness I needed—anointed confirmation, as if he whispered: "You saw just what you thought you saw."

Now you can slam the book or flip the page right here. Or, you can read along and think, like I do, "Hmm, heaven even comes to ordinary plain-folk."

I'm no saint, but I'm now among the ones who've had a dream. Who carry it with us wherever we go from that day forth.

I carried that dream with me when I crisscrossed this country, for two months, long ago, looking for the faces—and the stories—of those who were poor, who were hungry. I carried it, day in and day out, as I poked around the city where I live and work, where, one holiday season, I collected stories of the neediest of needy folk for my newspaper. Walked into apartments way up high in dingy high-rises and narrowly made it out of one not-so-friendly two-flat where there hadn't been a speck of heat in weeks, and where someone who huddled there made it abruptly very clear that I was not welcome, not at all. I certainly carried that dream back in the days when I was a nurse, a nurse who cared for—and loved—kids with cancer, and every time I stepped to a bedside, I looked into eyes like the ones on the Cross.

I carry the dream now, in the leafy town where I live, where, ironically, it's harder to keep the dream alive because no one on the surface looks so needy, few let on to deep-down aching. Everyone is cleaned, is polished. Children carry smartphones and tablets. Play games on glowing little screens while they wait for lessons that cost, for half an hour, what some families pay for a whole week's groceries. I've learned, though, not to mistake manicured for sated, not in ways that matter.

I even hold tight to the dream—or I try anyway—when it tests me: when some roadster at a red light blares his horn at me, because I've dared to wait for green. When a kid down the block leaves someone's little one off the birthday party list—and doesn't bother trying to keep it quiet.

We all need the dream; we all need it deeply.

Fact is, the only thing to do if we've lived a dream is to wake up every morning and tuck it in our pocket, take it where we go. Try, day after soul-grating day, to not give up, to not let down the dream. Not let the phone call go unmade, or the unkind word go uncorrected.

It is the pulse beat, really, of our every day. It is the undying belief that it is here, at our kitchen tables, in our front halls, and our workrooms, that the dream puts on its clothes. Takes on flesh and bone and matter in our every blessed hour.

The dream is in where we choose to send our children out to play. It is how we cook, and who we choose to feed. It is in the people we invite into our homes, the stories we ask them to tell, so our children can listen, can soak up sparks of wisdom that come from far beyond our walls. It is how we look into the eye of the guy pumping gas, or the pink-haired checker ringing up our groceries. And how and where we toil. It is in the getting up on Sunday morning and going out to someplace where the lessons come from far wiser teachers, instead of staying huddled round the table, flipping through the news, keeping watch of birds.

It is, day in and day out, saying to yourself: *I have a dream. I see a world other than the one before me. It starts, right now, with my next whole breath.*

Blessed Be January

In the Christian liturgical calendar the year opens amid the twelve days of Christmas, not long after the Nativity. In distant darkness, the brightest star blinks on, drawing the wisest journeyers. Epiphany. And so unfold the depths of Christmastide. In the hushed wake of those astonishments comes Ordinary Time, a time to behold quotidian wonders. To celebrate the miracle of the unheralded everyday, to lift up those unadorned hours of our lives that beg no attention but quietly, certainly, invite in the sacred. In the Hebrew calendar, it won't be long till Tu B'Shevat, the Jewish new year of the trees, when, in mid-winter in Israel, the almond tree awakes from its winter's slumber. In the holy land where all of these blessings begin, it's the date on the calendar when vernal whisperings begin. Jewish scholar Abraham Joshua Heschel instructs us to be attached to the holiness of time, to be attached to sacred events, "to learn how to consecrate sanctuaries that emerge from the magnificent stream of the year."

A Count-Your-Blessings Calendar

Fourteen Blessings for January

Here, fourteen blessings, a short-course curriculum in paying attention, slowing time, fine-tuning your gaze on the gifts of the season of deepening stillness. Some are tied to particular dates, others might be sprinkled throughout the month, all are in hopes of awakening you to the astonishments and wonder of the newborn year. All are calls to the holy.

New Year's Day (Jan. 1): Usher in the new year with a day of quietude; sunrise to sundown, hushed. Unplug. Slow simmer. Amble. May the loudest utterance be the turning of a page. Or the murmur of a tender kiss.

Blessing 2: Weather lesson: In life, we are wise to keep ourselves stocked deep inside with whatever it takes to weather all that life throws our way. It is resilience with which we must line our inner shelves. And unswerving faith, stored in gallon jugs, to ride out any storm.

Epiphany (Jan. 6): Bundle up and take a moonwalk. Consider the gift of the nightlight that waxes and wanes but always guides our way. Pay attention to the moon's portion. Keep a moon journal, recording each night's lunar fraction, on the way toward wholeness or decline. What blessing, especially for a child. Isn't this the miracle of learning to marvel?

Blessing 4: There is something mystical about the drama of a winter storm. You can't help but feel small as the sky turns marbled gray, the winds pick up, howl. Trees commence their thrashing. It's a fine thing for the human species to remember the amplitude of what we're up against.

Blessing 5: Take extra care to scatter cracked corn, peanut butter-smeared pine cones, and suet cakes for the loyal backyard critters who've settled in for winter, especially when arctic winds screech. Whisper thanks for those who keep watch on us.

Blessing 6: Proffer consecration for the scarlet-cloaked cardinal—the one flash of pigment till Valentines flutter. He is the very heartbeat of promise, hope on a wing, a laugh-out-loud reminder that we are not alone. That red of reds shatters all that's bleak, shouts: "There is life where you are doubting."

Rev. Dr. Martin Luther King Jr.'s Birthday (Jan. 15): Read the whole of Dr. King's "I Have a Dream" speech. Picture the world as you would dream it, then set out to make it real, one act of kindness at a time.

Blessing 8: Inhale this hope for today, and every tomorrow thereafter: "We can, to a certain extent, change the world; we can work for the oasis, the little cell of joy and peace in a harried world. We can throw our pebble in the pond and be confident that its ever-widening circle will reach around the world. We repeat, there is nothing we can do but love, and, dear God, please enlarge our hearts to love each other, to love our neighbor, to love our enemy as well as our friend."—Dorothy Day, American journalist, social activist, founder of the Catholic Worker Movement, someday saint (1897–1980).

Blessing 9: Keep watch on the night-by-night waxing of the moon. Treat yourself to midnight's moon lace. Tiptoe to a window—or straight under heaven's dome. When the moon is nearly full, behold the moonbeams as they spill. All the earth, in dappled shadow. Better than Chantilly, sure to take your breath away.

Blessing 10: Sometimes we walk in circles before we find our way—or at least I do. Maybe the way forward is threaded by wonder. Maybe the place to begin—and this is the season for new beginnings—is right here where we are. Maybe the way to begin is to be as still as we can possibly be, to plunge ourselves into those places where wonder can't help but brush up against us. But to notice, to pay attention, we need to go quiet. To still the noise. Quell the cacophony. Go to the woods or the edge of the shore. Go to where the waters rush or trickle or flow in and flow out. Stand under the stars of a cold winter's night. We're wrapped in the holiest text, the calligraphy of the great Book of Nature, God's first book, the ancient and timeless antidote to the madness of civilization. Where do you find wonder?

Blessing 11: Hibernation, it seems, is hard-wired into our winter selves. We're wise to reach beyond the confines of our cave. Dial up a friend. Set the tea kettle to whistling. Bask in the illumination of poet-philosopher Mark Nepo, who reminds: "Nothing compares to the sensation of being alive in the company of another. It is God breathing on the embers of our soul."

Blessing 12: Startle at the newborn day. Wrap yourself in the sanctuary of stillness. A morning like this, I often think, is the closest God comes to putting a finger to lips, whispering, *Shhhhhhhh. Be still. Open your ears, open your soul. Drink. Drink in the stillness, the quiet, the pause. This dawn, this start to the day, is reminder: the holiest sound in the whole wide world is the sound of just listening.* What do you hear?

Blessing 13: "Attentiveness is the natural prayer of the soul." —Nicolas Malebranche, French Oratorian priest and rationalist philosopher (1638-1715).

Blessing 14: "Contemplation is life itself, fully awake, fully active, fully aware that it is alive. It is spiritual wonder. It is spontaneous awe at the sacredness of life, of being. It is gratitude for life." —Thomas Merton, Trappist monk, mystic, writer (1915-1968).

The January Kitchen:

As the curtain rises on the newborn year, we find ourselves tucking away tins, now emptied of all but the last sweet crumbs, vestige of merriment, of splurge upon splurge.

Hibernation—an old-fashioned word for *hygge* (that *au courant* Danish term for "cozy comforts")—beckons. Which might be why depth of winter is the season that draws me closest to the cookstove. I practically purr puttering around the kitchen. All-day pots bubble away, lulling me into dreamy meditative fugues. Slow cooking, I'd wager, was made for snowy days, stay-inside days. Doughs rise. Wine-steeped stews simmer. Chowders thicken. Fruity compotes collapse into jewel-toned ooze. It's all a plethora of stove-top seduction, as what you pitch into the pot gives way, a few hours in, to heat and spice and saintly patience. It's kitchen adagio, the slow dance of surrender. And at the cookstove, trophies come dolloped on fork or soupspoon. Either way, you won't want to dash too soon.

Proper Porridge

I stand at the cookstove, stirring. And stirring. And stirring. Five minutes, maybe seven, bent in prayer. For that's what seems to happen every time I stand there, spoon in hand, circles upon circles lifeguarding the oats.

Oats + water + salt.

That's the equation. Quite simple. All the rest is alchemy, and stirring. Oats in the morning—oats done properly, I've found—unfold the day in slow time. Meditative time. If ever the cookstove becomes prayer altar it is at the dawn, when the house is only beginning its morning grunts and hisses and shivers and burps. When the kitchen is dark except for the flame of the burner and the single bulb that casts its faint beam on my pot.

I didn't used to stand at attention, not for so long a stir anyway. But then I went to Londontown, and one chilly morning I found a plump pot of porridge standing sentry on a shelf at a cozy corner cafe. I admit to being charmed by the name—*porridge* (poetic, with a hint of the ancient, the Celtic, perhaps; and as opposed to the more plebeian, American *oatmeal*)—as much as the contents lumped inside.

Then I dipped in my spoon. And what I tasted was pure

soothe. If food has the capacity to sandpaper the rough spots of our soul—and I believe it most certainly does—then that first spoonful of proper British porridge declared itself "necessary balm." Balm begging to begin the day, every day. Or at least the ones when fortification is needed. When what lies ahead in the hours to come just might fell you, buckle your knees. And those of all the ones you love, the ones still dreamy in their beds.

While swirling the velvety porridge there in my mouth, I noticed the words on the cardboard tub in which the porridge was served. Again, a call to attention.

Here's what I read: "Well worth the wait: Porridge is a surprisingly tricky dish to perfect (it's taken us years to get ours right). Stirring is good. Boiling is bad. Slowly, slowly simmering is the key. You just can't rush a good porridge. So we don't."

It was cooking instruction as *koan*, as *kenshu* (Buddhist notions, both; the former a teaching, often a paradox or puzzle, prompting deeper enlightenment, the latter a way of seeing).

And it captured my attention, all right.

Worth-the-Wait Porridge

When your morning prayer on a particular day—a day that demands much, too much, from its players—seems most aptly punctuated by the stirring of spoon through a muddle of oats. When the first thing you reach for, come dawn, is the grain that amounts to a mother's amulet. And as you stand there tossing in handfuls of shriveled-up gems—fruits the colors of amethyst, ruby, garnet, or onyx—you imagine yourself some sort of sorceress, arming your brood for the slaying of dragons to come.

Provenance: Nigel Slater + Felicity Cloake + The Ballymaloe Cookbook

Yield: 2 bowls, or 1 if you find yourself famished after a long night's nap

   1 cup rolled or steel-cut oats*
   3 cups water**
   ¼ teaspoon salt
   Assorted accoutrements: dried cranberries, apricots,
      raisins; sliced banana, chunks of apple; handfuls of
      almonds or walnuts; a spoon of peanut or almond
      butter; a sprinkling of wheat germ; a drizzle of honey
      or molasses; a spoonful of brown sugar. (Any of these

would likely leave a porridge purist aghast, but some mornings a bit of rabble-rousing is the order of the day.)

* Porridge *cognoscenti* all prescribe Flahavan's Irish Porridge Oats, if you're aiming for indescribable deliciousness.

** While water is traditional—in fact, *The Scots Kitchen*, F. Marian McNeill's recently republished 1929 classic, recommends spring water—porridge is sometimes made with hot milk, although that might mark you as a sybarite.

1. After culling dozens of porridge recipes, I've determined that all the enlightened porridgers subscribe to a quick toasting of the oats, a mere minute or two in a dry porridge pot over medium heat, until faintly golden. (If you choose steel-cut oats, or a mix of rolled and steel-cut, you'll want to soak the steel-cut bits overnight, after pouring boiling water, in three-to-one ratio, water to oats, atop the oats and parking them off in the corner. Put the lid on the pot, and bid them goodnight.)

2. Next morning, or when your belly's growling for that proper porridge, add water to oats in the pot (unless you've gone for the overnight soak), or if you prefer your oats creamier, make it milk or even cream. Whichever your pleasure, keep to that three-to-one fluid-to-oats ratio, your golden ratio here. (If you've opted for the all-night immersion, you might need to add just a glug of water or milk in the morning so your oatsy bits are sufficiently

aswim. But after a long night's idle, your steel-cut bits likely will need little but heat at this point. And fret not: oats might be the original forgiving grain.)

3. Stir, on low heat. A good five to ten minutes, please. Yes, stirring without pause—long, slow, meditative circles with your wooden spoon, or spurtle, a flat wooden stirring utensil designed by the Scots in the fifteenth century to keep oats from going lumpy, but of course. (Opines Mr. Slater: "Stirring is essential if the porridge is to be truly creamy.")

4. Add salt after porridge has been cooking for a good five to ten minutes. (Again, notes Nigel: "If the salt is introduced too early, it can harden the oats. Porridge needs cooking for longer than you think if the starch is to be fully cooked.")

5. Put the lid on your porridge pot and remove from the heat. Allow the velvety mound to breathe deeply and surrender to its steamy confines. A five-minute rest at a minimum. There is simply no hurrying a porridge of proper production.

6. Ladle into your favorite bowl, douse with a splash of fresh, cold milk, and adorn with handfuls of whatever accoutrements brighten your morning. Or to put it as the British food scribe Felicity Cloake so poetically puts it in *The Guardian* of London (and why wouldn't you want to put it thusly?): "A girdle of very cold milk, or single cream on special occasions, is essential . . . but a knob of butter, while melting attractively into the oats, proves too greasy for my taste."

Elixir Pudding

Excuse me while we interrupt our regularly scheduled programming to bring you the following emergency announcement: you must, I mean must, go directly to where you keep your bread that is old, that is galloping swiftly toward stale.

You must grab it before it goes straight down the hill. Now rip it in bits. Big bits are fine, if that's the bit of your choosing. Little bits work as well. As do bits somewhere in the middle.

We are en route to bread pudding, that soft, mushy pillow of succor, the one with the cinnamon-sugary crust, providing just the right edge to your puff. The pudding of which one ample spoonful turns us all back into tots.

You'll be aswirl, at the very first taste, in visions of nurseries and prams and old English nannies, with considerable bosoms, leading you on with a ladle. Or, you'll simply swallow and hum.

The reason we're rushing is this: the recipe I concocted, with a little help from Mark Bittman, he who teaches us how to cook everything, seems to have cast a sort of spell. I think it's a pudding possessed.

So much so, I must proselytize, attempt to persuade you. My little one, who spooned it up for dessert, then again before bedtime, and then, not twelve hours later, once more for breakfast, looked at me dreamy-eyed from under his curls and inquired: "Will you make it for Christmas?"

And the firstborn, so inspired was he, he sent me a love note (yes, a pudding-y love note): "The pudding was great. I needed it today. Life wouldn't be worth living without such a home to come to. I really mean it. Love, love, love."

What I want to know is, who mixed the elixir in with the eggs and the butter and bread-on-the-verge-of-bread-crumbing?

I saw no one there in the kitchen, but some invisible hooligan must have been fooling with me and my bread bits. What happened is this: there I was, minding my start-of-week business, when suddenly I heard a whisper from there in the corner, from the basket where tired old bread sits before dying.

"Come, come," it called. I swear that it did.

And before I knew it, I was off to the bookshelf, hauling down my old friend Mr. Bittman. Right there, on page 662 of his tome, bread pudding in three easy steps. So I followed instructions, then I vamped—made it my elixir bread pudding. I grated some apple into my pudding. I tossed in whole fistfuls of raisins. And I dusted the top with a bumper crop of cinnamon and vanilla-infused sugar.

And the results, as I mentioned, were utterly stunning. Never before seen.

To come up with something that had my boys so starry-eyed, well, that is a day to press to the heart. May the coos and the star-dazzled eyes be many at your house.

Elixir (Bread) Pudding

When a pouf of billowy sweetness is called for, when you're inclined to pull from the oven a golden-domed cloud of the original comfort foodstuffs: bread + milk + sugar + eggs. Isn't that the nursery maid's tried and true prescription, the one sure cure for whenever life pummels in hard-to-take blows? And doesn't the deep of winter sometimes insist on supersize doses of comfort, most emphatically perched on the end of a spoon?

Provenance: Mark Bittman's How to Cook Everything *+ imagination, my own*

Yield: 1 batch, or 6 servings

3 cups milk

4 tablespoons unsalted butter, plus some for greasing the pan

1½ teaspoons cinnamon, divided

½ cup plus 1 tablespoon sugar, divided (I make a habit
of burying a vanilla pod in my sugar canister, so my
white sugar is always infused with Tahitian vanilla
notes)

¼ teaspoon salt

Best day-old bread you can find (Mr. Bittman calls for
8 slices; I reached for the remains of a loaf of *challah*,
the braided egg bread we bring to the table for
every Shabbat)

3 eggs

1 apple, grated

1 or 2 fistfuls raisins, cranberries, or your choice from
the dried-fruits department

1. Preheat oven to 350 degrees Fahrenheit. Over low heat in a saucepan, warm milk, butter, 1 teaspoon cinnamon, ½ cup sugar, and salt, just until butter melts. Meanwhile, butter a 1½-quart baking dish or 8-inch square pan. Cut and tear bread into bite-size bits.

2. Place bread in baking dish. Pour hot, buttery milk over it. Sigh as you pour. Let milk sit for a bit, occasionally dunking any recalcitrant bits not willing to tread milk. Beat the eggs and stir into bread mixture. Add 1 cup grated, drained apple and handful of raisins. Mix remaining cinnamon and sugar, and sprinkle over the top. Set the baking dish into a larger baking pan and pour hot water into the pan to within an inch of the top of the dish. (You're indulging your pudding-filled dish in an oven-y steam bath.)

3. Bake 45 minutes to 1 hour, or until a thin-bladed knife comes clean from the center; center should be just a bit wobbly. Run under the broiler for about 30 seconds to get that yummy golden-brown crust. Serve warm or cold. With whipped cream. Keeps well for two days covered in the refrigerator, but I don't think it'll stick around even half that long. It never lingers at our house.

When All Else Fails . . . Turn to Page 200

A quarter century ago, when I was plotting my firstborn's second birthday fete, I flipped open the pages of my monthly infusion of delicious, *Gourmet* magazine, and landed on page 200. Since then, that page has pretty much been my no-fail, last-ditch, best-hope-of-filling-a-hole-in-a-heart-by-way-of-the-belly cookery map. After twenty-five years, the magazine's binding is coming unglued, the page now crusted with splatters of *roux*. No matter; by now, I know my way. Nearly by heart. It's a page that plies its magic any day, really, in any season, but especially so on a cold wintry day, when the sunlight is waning. And so it was, on plenty a day in the growing-up years, when the boy who'd loped to the car at the schoolhouse curb was a boy with a much-leaden heart.

On just such a day, I'd reach for my holy salvation: the plainly named "Baked Macaroni and Cheese," à la page 200. It's a cheesy-buttery bath stirred round and through tubes of wide-mouthed pasta, each tube filling with ooze as much as being wrapped in it. It vies, in our house, with bread pudding as the neck-and-neck numbers one and two comforts on a spoon.

Over the years, the making of it—for me, anyway—is as soothing as it must be for my boys to polish it off in one sitting. Assembling its components—the butter, cheddar, flour, milk, salt, paprika, bread crumbs, and Parmesan shavings to finish it off—I slip into priestess mode. My old black cookstove—an industrial-grade contraption that somehow slipped into this old house in the 1970s, never to be removed—is my altar.

I begin my incantations and prestidigitations right there, where the flame is cranked, and the concoctions in my pots begin to bubble, not unlike vats of heavenly potions. With the oven cranked to 375, the kitchen begins to warm. Everything about this kitchen ritual is warming. Soon, my old sweater is off, and as I stir I imagine my sweet boys coming home to find the big white ceramic soufflé dish perched atop the stove.

Is there a more certain way to say I love you than to have cooked all afternoon? To have reached for the cookery shelf and pulled out the one thing a kid asks for on those nights when his sleepy head hits the pillow but the worries won't be extinguished?

Cure-All Mac and Cheese

When the bee stings, or the homesick blues need quelling, this oozy spoonful of deliciousness belongs in a mama's tin of kitchen cure-alls. It's the ubiquitous remedy at our house for any ailment in the book. (And one or two make-believe ones, besides.) And it's just what the doctor orders for frosty-cheeked rascals fresh in from the cold.

Provenance: Gourmet *magazine, May 1995*

Yield: Serves 8 children

> 3 tablespoons unsalted butter
> 3 ½ tablespoons all-purpose flour
> ½ teaspoon paprika
> 3 cups whole milk
> 1 teaspoon salt
> ¾ pound pasta, tubes or wagon wheels or whatever shape suits your fancy (a tube—penne or rigatoni, among the many—fills with the cheesy sauce and makes a fine, pillowy bite)
> 10 ounces sharp cheddar cheese, shredded coarse (about 2 ¾ cups)

1 cup fresh bread crumbs, coarse

¼ cup (or more) Parmesan shavings

1. Preheat oven to 375 degrees Fahrenheit and butter a 2-quart shallow baking dish (the broader the crust, the better).

2. In a 6-quart pot, bring 5 quarts salted water to a boil for cooking pasta.

3. In a heavy saucepan, melt butter over moderately low heat, and stir in flour and paprika. Cook roux, whisking, 3 minutes; then whisk in milk and salt. Bring sauce to a boil, whisking, and simmer, whisking occasionally, 3 minutes. Remove pan from heat.

4. Stir pasta into pot of boiling water and boil, stirring occasionally, until *al dente*. Drain pasta in a colander, and in a large bowl stir together pasta, sauce, and 2 cups cheddar cheese. Transfer mixture to prepared dish. *Macaroni and cheese may be prepared up to this point 1 day ahead and chilled, covered tightly (an indispensable trick when confronting a serious to-do list for a day of, say, birthday or holiday jollity).*

5. In a small bowl, toss remaining ¾ cup cheddar with bread crumbs and sprinkle over pasta mixture, topping it all with a downpour of Parmesan shavings (a heavy hand with the cheese is never a bad thing, certainly not at my house where my boys insist I do so, preferring their cheese to supersede bread crumbs).

6. Bake macaroni and cheese, uncovered, in middle of oven for 25 to 30 minutes, or until golden and bubbling. Let stand 10 minutes before serving. At last: dig in.

Beef Stew with Pomegranate Seeds, Nestled Beside Aromatic Rice

The very definition of winter cookery, this aromatic number came to me from a friend who belongs among the Jazz Queens of the Kitchen. She works the stove the way Ella Fitzgerald climbed the scales, with that rare dose of confidence and cool that allows for riffing, zigging when all else might zag. You give my dear and soulful friend Susan a chord, a launching pad from which to soar—in this case, beef and pomegranate—and she takes flight. Her first rendition of the recipe read like musical notations, scribbled in the margins of the page. The barest wisps of what to do, yet grounded in seamless fluency. She knows nuance by heart, and thus can play where others toil. Cooking with Susan—or following along her kitchen notes—is pure entertainment on a long cold winter's afternoon. And the star turn at the table will bring on thunderous applause.

Provenance: This dollop of winter wonder arose from the vast imagination of kitchen wunderkind, Susan Faurot.

Prep time: 20 minutes, if beef is butcher-trimmed and you're lucky enough to find pre-plucked pomegranate seeds in your produce aisle (increasingly likely, as the pluses of the seeded superfruit are trumpeted round the world).

Baking time: 2 hours

Yield: 4 to 6 servings

2 pounds beef chuck, cut into cubes

Salt and pepper, to taste

2 tablespoons olive oil

2 to 3 cloves garlic, chopped

1 teaspoon ground cumin

1 pound pearl onions, skinned

2 to 4 stalks of celery, sliced thinly

5 bay leaves

Several sprigs of thyme

1 cup red wine

1 cup pomegranate juice (unsweetened)

$\frac{1}{3}$ cup chopped walnuts

$\frac{1}{2}$ cup pomegranate seeds

1. Preheat oven to 300 degrees Fahrenheit.

2. Salt and pepper beef chunks. In a large skillet or Dutch oven, brown the beef in 2 tablespoons olive oil; don't overcook, just brown all sides.

3. If you've used a skillet, transfer to Dutch oven (or large baking dish with a lid). Otherwise, stick with the Dutch oven, and save yourself—or your sous chef—a bit of pot scrubbing.

4. Toss browned beef chunks with chopped garlic and cumin; add onions, celery, bay leaves, thyme. Cook for two minutes, or until vapors convince you the magic's begun. Toss again, then pour in red wine and pomegranate juice.

5. Cover and place on middle rack in the oven. Bake 2 hours.

6. When done, remove sprigs of thyme and bay leaves. Garnish with chopped walnuts and pomegranate seeds, those garnet gems. Add chopped parsley, if you please. Finally, as the recipe title instructs, nestle alongside Aromatic Rice. (Or, should you prefer, break loose and blanket your rice with the beef. Such are the liberations to be found in the kitchen.)

Aromatic Rice

When cooking your rice (approximately 1½ to 2 cups of uncooked rice), per instructions, add the following (along, of course, with cooking water):

2-inch stick of cinnamon
2 to 3 whole cloves
2 to 3 green cardamom pods, cracked

You'll be transported to a magical someplace, far off in the Land of Deliciousness . . .

Winter Salad: Roasted Fennel, Red Onion, and Orange

Amid the unrelenting grip of winter, be it endless swirls of falling snow, or unbroken monochrome days, there's something particularly invigorating about a wintry salad that might be mistaken for a painterly still life. A pastiche of amethyst, and celadon, and burnt sunset orange. It's the oven that works its magic here, scooping a humble trio from the fruit and vegetable bins, revamping it into a showcase so fine you might be inclined to inhale it till Easter. The alchemists in the kitchens at *Food52*, a test-kitchen-approved community cooking site, put it best, when they described it thusly (invoking a wee bit of Borscht Belt, in what sounds like the lead-in to a culinary zinger): "Three winter standbys—an orange, an onion, and a fennel bulb—walk into an oven together, and morph into a warm winter salad that virtually dresses itself." Dresses beautifully, yes; better yet, it's sublimely delicious.

Provenance: Inspired by Molly Stevens, adapted from All About Roasting: A New Approach to A Classic Art + Food52

Yield: Serves 4

1 large or 2 small fennel bulbs (about 1 pound
    untrimmed)
1 medium red onion
1 small navel orange, scrubbed
2 tablespoons extra-virgin olive oil, plus more for
    drizzling
Kosher salt and freshly ground pepper

1. Preheat oven to 400 degrees Fahrenheit. Line a rimmed baking
   sheet with parchment paper (this'll keep your oranges from sticking
   to the pan).

2. Trim the fronds (frilly ends and stems) from fennel. Stand a bulb
   on its base and cut in half lengthwise, from core to stem. Using
   a paring knife, remove most of the core from each half. Now, cut
   crosswise into ¼-inch-thick crescent-shaped slices. Toss onto the
   baking sheet, and repeat if you're using two fennels. (Don't toss
   out the fronds of your fennel; they'll add a festive frilly dash on
   your way to the table.)

3. Cut onion in half, from root to stem. Peel and remove the root end
   from both halves. Slice onion halves crosswise into ¼-inch-thick
   half-moons, and toss in with the fennel.

4. Next, slice about 1½ inches off each end of the orange and
   reserve (you'll use these later to squeeze over the salad). Stand
   the orange on one cut end and cut lengthwise in half; next, cut

each half lengthwise again, leaving you with 4 pieces. Arrange each quarter, cut side down, and slice crosswise into ¼-inch-thick quarter-moon-shaped pieces.

5. Add the orange to fennel and onion. Drizzle olive oil on top; season well with salt and plenty of pepper. Here's where you make like a hands-on mix-master: Toss to coat, trying not to fling bits about the kitchen, and spread in an even layer on the baking sheet (if it's too crowded, it all gets steamed rather than golden-roasted).

6. Slide sheet pan onto center rack of the oven. Roast, stirring with a spatula after 15 minutes, and again every 10 minutes or so. The vegetables close to the edge of the pan brown more quickly than those in the center, so stirring and shaking the pan helps everything cook at the same rate. Continue roasting until the vegetables and orange are tender and the outer edges begin to caramelize, anywhere from 25 to 45 minutes.

7. Transfer to a platter or bowl (a wide shallow one works well, but really it's delicious no matter your vessel). Let cool for at least 15 minutes, or to room temperature. Then bring on what amounts to liquid sunshine: Squeeze the juice from one of the reserved orange ends over the salad. Taste. If needed, add a pinch of salt and squeeze the other orange piece over it. Drizzle with a wee bit of your best olive oil, and serve warm or at room temperature. Before you ferry your vibrant mound to the table, grab a few of those tucked-away un-roasted fennel fronds (the ones you saved up above). Ceremonially—and with requisite aplomb—adorn your roasted heap of wintry deliciousness. A little frill never hurts.

Winter's Wonderlist

January

snow-laden sky creeping in unawares . . .

the red-cheeked badge of courage, come the close of a slow-spooled walk through winter's woods . . .

frost ferns on the windowpanes . . .

snow falling first in feather-tufts, then fairy-dusted stars, and, finally, prodigiously, in what could only be curds . . .

noses pressed to glass, keeping watch as winter's storm wallops . . .

soup kettle murmuring—slow, steady, hungrily . . .

scribble your own here:

February

Just when you're starting
to think the unfurling of
the eventual daffodil is
pure fiction and folly,
that red bird of courage
belts out from on high.

February Field Notes:

Full Snow Moon, or Hunger Moon, casts its midnight shadows on the drifts and mounds that, traditionally, measure deepest of the year.

❄ While Earth—at least up north—is deeply blanketed, the heavens shine at their brightest with the night sky's number one light: Sirius, the Dog Star, which twinkles from the shoulder of Orion's Great Dog (Canis Major). The star's name means "scorcher," and its luminosity is twenty-two times greater than the sun.

❄ Undaunted by snow—and under the sparkle of big-dog star—the Great Horned Owl, amorous just last month, now settles onto her clutch of eggs; it's brood time already. Tufted titmice and cardinals take their cue and join in the mating game. So too, raccoon, woodchuck, beaver, skunk, and opossum.

❋ Early bluebirds find their way, once again, to the Eastern United States. Red-winged blackbirds, one of the most abundant birds in North America, flap back home if they've wintered in warmer climes; the frontline of spring's migration.

February is laden with clues, clues to keep us believing. If only we pause to pay closest attention.

February: Stirring Within

February is the month when we're wise to put our ear to the heartbeat all around. There's stirring deep beneath the crust of earth, and deep within our weary selves—invisible but certain.

Might that be the boiled-down essence of February's lesson? Faith in the notion that all is a work-in-progress, even when it's beyond our perception. Earthly and otherwise.

February tries its darnedest to turn us into doubters. Who says the days upon days of dreary will draw to an end? What if we're stuck in the midst of eternal winter? What if we never unclench from our own tight coils?

Oh, ye, of wobbling certitude: dial up your faith—and your fine-tuned antennae. February is laden with clues, clues to keep us believing. If only we pause to pay closest attention. Crouch down for keener inspection. Listen close, for the first stirrings of winter loosening its grip, making room for the light to seep in.

Perk your ear to the morning song of the cardinal, high in the treetops. Just when you're starting to think the unfurling of the eventual daffodil is pure fiction and folly, that red bird of courage belts out from on high. He's all but yodeling: *Do not despair, there is reason for hope*. Sunlight, like a fine Earl Gray left to steep in a fat-bellied teapot, grows stronger and truer minute by minute. And the cardinal, hard-wired to read the precise slant of the sun, knows before we do that just beyond this dreary horizon, the season of hope is arising.

So, too, the tips of the branches. Barely discernible bundles of bud, leaves clasped in prayer I've sometimes imagined, bulk up by the day, sometimes by the hour. Unless you have X-ray eyes, you'll not yet see quiverings on the crust of the earth. All the work there is deep underground, as with our soul.

Here's a little-known wonder of the second month of the year, the month named for Februalia, the Roman festival of purification: the Hebrew calendar pauses to soak in, to shout joy for these not-so-far-off vernal whisperings. It's called Tu B'Shevat, the Festival of the New Trees, and it's said to be the day when God decides how bountiful the fruit of each tree will be in the coming year. In Israel, it's when the almond tree awakes from its winter sleep, erupting in clouds of tissue-white flowers, the first

blossom of spring. Sixteenth-century Jewish mystics, known as the kabbalists, believed that we elevate ourselves by the eating of certain fruits—ten in all, fig, persimmon, pomegranate, among them—on Tu B'Shevat. If done with holy intention, they taught, sparks of light hidden in the fruit could be broken open from their shells, freed to float up to heaven, completing the circle of the renewal of life.

Oh my. You needn't be Jewish to want to drop to your knees. To bow down to the breathtaking, invisible knowing that the rhythms of heaven and earth unfold according to Divine ordination. And the shifting of season—our own and that of the cosmos—is blessing beyond blessing. One we're wise to read ever so closely. And in which to hold faith.

Why I Won't
Give Up on February

It is, of all the stretches here of days, the one that, like a testy child, pushes you pretty much to the precipice, to the urge to pack it up, move into some secret closet, turn out the lights and stew a while.

Perhaps, like Mr. Ground Hog, you'll peek out from time to time, catch the gloomy sky, dart back to where the coats dangle, and the boots convene a convention of vacuum-busting dust balls.

Perhaps you'll hear the snow fall, for the umpteen-millionth day in a row, and you'll want to pull your hair out.

Or, perhaps, you'll go on cold strike: saunter out to get the mail in just some skimpy little t-shirt, and shorts. Forego the knee-high rubber wellies. Do strappy sandals instead. Show skin. And what you're made of. Give those neighbors as big a shock as hearts can handle in the month of gooey chocolates stuffed in frilly, foil, heart-shaped boxes.

You can grouse, from now till thaw, about the unrelenting march of spirit-beating weather.

Like me when learning how to drive (a stick-shift on a busy highway, but that's a story for another day), the weather here is apt to lurch. Might wrench your neck, jerking back and forth from all the scribbles, dots, and dashes on the weather map.

Oh, my, what's that funnel running through the Tennessee Valley? Oh, no, what's with ice in Cincinnati, city of the seven hilly hills? And here, in sweet Chicago, get your neck brace on: one day cold and snowy. The next day colder still. Followed by rain that might as well come down in cubes, for the way it freezes, turns to sheets of call-the-orthopod, I-think-I-broke-my-tailbone.

Or, you can snuff the protest, leave the grumpy room. You can, if you care to, join my club. It's a club for contrarians. We like what no one else does. Cloudy days? We'll take 'em.

Thunderstorms? Bring on the cracks of lightning, riveting the sky. Stirring wonder in the way the trees show up like X-rays there against the stormy night.

I don't even mind all this: the diamond-dusted world I just woke up to. The way the flakes caught bits of moonlight, shimmered like a thousand million stars, scattered on the folds and folds and mounds and mounds of white.

I don't mind how papa cardinal, my red-bird joy especially in winter, I don't mind one bit how he sticks out against the snow. How he catches my breath. Fluffed up on branches, trying to beat the cold with his feathers perched at full attention. There he is just now, right outside my window, and the sun is barely up. He is the lone flash of pigment till the valentines begin. And when they're tucked away, papa still will strut his scarlet, the very heartbeat of promise.

I dare you, I do, to catch the flight of fury-feathered cardinal in the thick of falling snow and not whisper, "Oh, dear, there's the flight from heaven, sent to stir my soul."

That bird to me is hope on wing. A laugh-out-loud reminder that we are not alone. It can be

unrelenting cold and white, and that red of
reds shatters the tableau. Bursts through
the hopelessness, shouts, There is life
where you are doubting.

And that, I think, is why I love this
month. It's the month of nearly
giving up. Of thinking you cannot make it one last time. It's
the month of thinking you'll be
quashed before it ever ends.

But then the holy hallelujah comes. The
red bird. The pure contentment of mere survival.
The steaming bowl of soup when you come in from
shoveling, you Sisyphean fool.

You think, perhaps, the thinkers were not thinking when
they made this month the shortest one? Of course, they were,
they understood. Although they were down in Rome, where I
doubt this month is much too awful. And don't even pay attention to those leaping years, when we get a one-day extra helping.
Oh, loathesome, you might say.

But not me.

I say, bring it on, this lull when winter settles in, sinks deep,
when February mucks around inside my very marrow. Proves
it's the boss and we are merely mortals. Mortals complete with
goosebumps.

I like a month that isn't mamby-pamby. You wanna be a winter month? Well, then, act like it.

I take my coffee undiluted. I fill my car with full-strength octane. I'll take February just the same.

If we have half an ounce of courage, now's the time to show it. Go ahead, take a walk. Fill your lungs with frozen air, a composition that defies mere physics.

Not one ounce of living worth its weight in rock salt comes without extracting some toll. Matters not if it's a season's change, or healing heartbreak. Matters not if your long haul is clocking many miles. Or believing in a hard-won dream.

If we long for warmer winds, we've two choices: stay locked in the closet waiting out the thaw, or step outside, and drink in what the shortest month has to offer. The chance to be wholly wide-awake to sparkling snow, rosy cheeks, and papa cardinal landed on your windowsill. Oh my. I'll take my February.

On ice, if you can spare some.

Survival, Astonishingly

The weather people soothe us now with reports that it's all of 9-without-a-minus-sign degrees. But the thermometer outside my kitchen window insists otherwise. It says 5, and not a micrometer higher. Either way, that's eons better than the -22, or 45 below with wind chill. And here along the windy shore of Lake Michigan, wind counts mightily. It always counts.

Our house the other night was burping. Or so it sounded. Every once in a while, through the night, a thud arose from who knows where.

Sounded to me like things were crashing to the roof. I got up to check out the window, to see if I could see a falling something, to see if ice chunks were hurling toward the house.

The next day's news brought word that those ominous noises—those noises that had people rushing to their windows, to see if glass had shattered, limbs had fallen, or maybe stars had tumbled from the heavens—those noises were a phenomenon known as "frost quakes." So defined as: "a seismic event that may be caused by a sudden cracking action in frozen soil or rock saturated with water or ice." Egad. Yet another quirk to be added to the February weather woes. Count me among the ones who do not like "seismic events" in and under and all around my house.

At our seismically-burping house, as we whirled into the abyss of the polar vortex, we settled our worries on anyone or anything who might, for some godforsaken reason, be stuck outside. We worried mightily about the folks who sleep in tents under viaducts and along the banks of the Chicago River, and in flimsy encampments near the railroad yards, in hollows of the city where the forgotten stake their claim in pockets of oblivion. We prayed that somehow someone might convince those folks to leave behind their propane tanks and blankets and the cardboard boxes they call home. And just for one night—or until the vortex whirled away—deign to climb aboard a warming bus, or a cot inside a shelter. Dear God, please do not let there be a child out there, I whispered over and over.

Closer to home—right outside our kitchen door, in fact—our heap of fears focused on the tiny feathered flocks who dart and flit all day, every day. We knew that we had blankets, and a fridge filled with clementines. And a tea kettle that could whistle on command. But what about the red birds? What about the little juncoes, those snow monks of the winter? And what about the sparrows, the unassuming brown birds whose chatter never stops.

If I could have, I would have opened wide the kitchen door, invited them all in. But I knew that was whimsy. Pure wishful whimsy. As if a flock of cardinals would roost above our dinner plates or huddle high up in the pantry. I was not alone in my worrying. The tall bespectacled fellow who shares this house, he's the one who first mentioned the little birds when we bowed our heads to pray before Tuesday night's dinner. He did the same on Wednesday and Thursday.

We could not for the life of us figure out how those tiny-footed creatures— the ones who weigh all of five aspirins or one and a half slices of bread (that's 1.5 ounces, the average lightness of being of any papa cardinal)—how in the world would those tiny wisps of heartbeat survive through the long dark arctic night?

It was an equation of survival stripped to its essence. It's not every night we boil it down to life or death, just beyond our kitchen window. And hope against hope for life to be the victor.

I couldn't bear to imagine the little things hovering, tucked away in some bough of some fir tree that hardly blocked the wind. I pictured tiny frozen red birds fallen to the snowdrifts by morning. I couldn't sleep.

Sometimes, it takes extremes—the severe storm warning, the daunting diagnosis, even the unreturned phone call from someone we worry about—to snap us out of our lethargies, our take-it-for-grantedness, to pull back the veil, to see in sharp focus just how fragile, how precarious, all of this is. Sometimes, the cold slap is just what we need to rise to deepest attention.

Once the daylight came, once the sun against the snow made it hurt to stare into the glare, we kept watch anyway. Nothing moved out there, save a snow-capped branch blowing in the wind. I'd trudged out early, dumped a can of seed—just in case. But nothing and no one budged. All day on the coldest day, the yard was still.

At last, one chickadee appeared. Darted toward the seed, nibbled, flitted off. But no one else. Then nightfall came again. And dawn. And nothing. Not a single bird.

And then, as I kept watch through the morn- ing, as the bespectacled one peered from his upstairs window, at 10:57 yesterday morning, there it came: the flash of muted red that is mama cardinal.

She clung to a branch not far from the feeder. And then, at last, she swooped in. As she pecked away at the sunflower seeds, along came her backup squad: one red bird, aka Papa, and two more mamas.

There was jubilance in our kitchen. The mere shock of red against the white-on-gray tableau, it was victorious. Nothing short of a death-defying feat. It was still, at that mid-day hour, -12 degrees. And yet, somehow, the little birds survived. Had made it through the wind-whipping night, had endured a cold they'd never ever known, and tucked away in some unknown-to-us cove, employing unimaginable survival skills. We should show such grit. We too should defy the insurmountable when it's heaped against us. For this, all this, I pray.

I stood in awe. The mysteries of the woodland escape and astonish me. The masterwork of creation is what floors me, over and over and over.

We've pummeled this holy earth, with our chimneys spewing smoke, and the poisons we've poured into the waters, and yet, on a polar vortex night, the papa cardinal clung on, he didn't freeze to death. He doubled the air mass in between his feathers. He slowed his breath. And before the mercury climbed to zero, he flashed across the yard. The red flash, triumphant.

Thank you, Great Protector. And hallelujah cardinals. And all who have survived.

Oranges-and-Chocolate Brigade

The louder the alerts on the radio about arctic wind chills and never-before lows, the more I got to thinking about frozen people, as in frozen by the cold. Folks with no choice about being in the cold.

What got me thinking were the folks I was passing as I made my way through the bone-chilling day. The crews cutting down trees, their arms and legs and hands stiffly moving as they hoisted their saws in their orange puffy suits. A fellow, red-cheeked, frost-bearded, standing in the middle of the road with a pole, measuring something that couldn't wait till a day with bearable temperatures.

I thought of the mail carriers, the garbage haulers, the firehose aimers. I thought of the crossing guards, the meter readers, the ruptured-water-main fixers. I thought of my friend who bundles up "like an Inuit," she says, and walks twenty minutes to work, her cheeks so numb she probably can't smile when she gets there, not for a good half hour.

Then I really got to thinking about frozen people. I started thinking about Dirt Man and Tax Man and Refrigerator Man. I thought about Shorty and Squeaky and a guy named Everett, who'd built himself a multiplex of boxes up on a platform so the rats couldn't get in, down in the bowels of the city, down under Lower Wacker Drive.

I met the whole civilization of under-street inhabitants a few years ago, when I tagged along with two saints, named Frank and Kay Fennell.

Frank and Kay do an amazing, uncomplicated thing: they flip open the trunk of their car, they fill it with boxes of home-cooked food, and every Thursday night, for a good twenty years, they drive to the depths of the city.

They cruise the streets of Lower Wacker, park, stick their heads around corners, poke behind pillars. They open their trunk, spoon hot food onto plates, pour glasses of water. They feed the hungry. And this time of year, they feed the near-frozen.

When the mercury drops this low, the airwaves get crowded with news bulletins. The folks who try to make the city stumble along, they beg the homeless to come in off the streets, off the sidewalks where they stretch out on a pile of flimsy blankets, inch as close as they can to the heating vents at the bases of shimmering towers.

But the good souls who call the streets home, they aren't much interested in leaving. They've got reasons aplenty why they can't stand the shelters. And if you ask questions, if you listen, you hear the pain, you hear the fear that keeps them locked where they are.

Too often, my first instinct when arctic winds hit is to hunker down, to draw into my cave. But sometimes, I told myself as I thought about frozen people, you need to dig beyond that. Sometimes you need to pull up your second instinct.

And that's when I hatched what you might think is a foolish idea.

But this world needs fools almost as much as it needs something else: the courage of plain old anybodies to get up, get out of their houses, walk up to a stranger, a cold, hungry stranger, hand him or her a brown paper bag, a bag filled with oranges and chocolate. And, just as certainly, the world needs folks with the solid conviction that if we don't notice the cold hungry stranger, if we don't let him or her know that he or she isn't forgotten, we might as well pack it up, call it a day, shut out the lights, and sign off the planet.

I call it the oranges-and-chocolate brigade.

My guardian angel in these matters, Kay Fennell, once told me: "We decided it was our job to sustain [these people] for whatever their next step would be. And that might be just to stay alive for the next twenty-four hours."

So I did what Kay would do: I went to the store, got oranges and Hershey's bars, Reese's cups, too. Grabbed a stash of brown bags and started to fill. I'm headed down to the bowels of the city, where Dirt Man and Tax Man were last seen on grubby old blankets inside torn cardboard boxes, desperately trying to keep their flesh and their blood at least half alive.

Before I even get there, I'll pass the men and boys who hawk newspapers in the middle of oncoming lanes. Or one of the folks who hovers at intersections, dodging green lights, with the signs clutched in raw, frozen fingers. "Homeless, please help."

It's not much, oranges and chocolate in a brown paper bag.

But it's fuel in the cold. And it might be something a little more than that.

It might say, in case anyone's listening, that we will not let the cold and the hungry lay down one more night thinking the world has forgotten, the world has gone heartless.

That's a lot to ask of plain oranges and chocolate. But if we don't ask, who will not wake—frozen, all through?

Here's the plot, simply: take a few lunch bags. Toss in oranges and chocolate, anything else that you fancy. Haul them to your car. You don't need to drive to the depths of the city to find cold folk. How about this: when you see someone out working, someone without much of a choice, roll down your window, stop your car. Reach out your arm, get out from behind the wheel even. Put your brown bag in his or her hand. Smile. Say what you will. Then go on your way. Or, be radical, invite that someone for a hot home-cooked dinner. Your choice. Always your choice.

When the Heavens
Bring Silence

The day was abuzz with the news: it was coming, beware! By twilight, the first shreds of evidence appeared—couldn't have been more gentle, scant flakes tumbling, liltingly caught in the porch light's corona. And the broadcasts blared on: this winter's big snow, enough snow to cancel the school bells, enough snow to bring on battalions of plows, it was coming. Children—especially a high schooler I know with a giant biology test slotted for the morrow—let out a whoop and slammed closed the textbooks. Meiosis and mitosis would have to wait.

I went to bed. With the blinds up because there is nothing I love so much as awaking to snow fall. No matter the hour. The earlier the better.

Sure enough, I awoke to the holiest sound I know: still silence. Not a peep or a plow. The barest whoosh of air swirling through snow-covered limbs. I stood there and drank it all in. Only now, an hour or so after the light seeped in, only now is the faint chorus of chirps beginning to stir Not a plow. Not a shovel. Not a footfall.

A morning like this, I often think, is the closest God comes to putting a finger to lips, whispering, *Shhhhhhhhh.*

Be still.

Open your ears, open your soul. Drink in the stillness, the quiet, the pause. Settle your soul. Put aside the rumblings that rumble. This dawn, this start to the day, is reminder: the holiest sound in the whole wide world is the sound of just listening. Remember to listen.

What do you hear?

It's prescriptive, a snowfall like this. Of all the choices in the meteorological tool kit, no other one comes with the soundtrack of silence. Except, I suppose, pure sunshine. But then, for me anyway, that comes with an undercoat of moaning. Too much sun and I start to wilt. I'll take a brisk pure snow any day.

I intend to listen all day. I intend to pull out the blankets and mugs. I intend to settle onto the couch with my very sweet boy who cannot escape. He's caught in the snow trap today. Everything is cancelled. Hallelujah!

Just now, a bolt of scarlet feather flashed by the window and settled down on the snow-mounded feeder. I took it as a call for breakfast—a bird call, that is—so I shoved my toes into boots and scooped up a can of sunflower seeds. It goes against my grain to unsettle snow, but I grabbed the shovel anyway— the cardinal was hungry, you see. And I shoveled myself a path. There's at least a foot of snow out there. And with more abandon than usual, I dumped. There is now black seed speckling my snow because I decided to share with the squirrels, and the big red fox should he decide to show up today. (He's been ambling by more and more often; the other morning, in fact, he curled up for a long winter's nap—a good three-quarters-of-an-hour nap—smack in the middle of the yard, circling this way and that till he found just the right lump for a pillow.)

And now, as the snow drips from my hair, the flakes out the window have plumped to double or triple their original size. No wonder, when we were little, we liked the idea that the angels were having a pillow fight. And the heavenly feathers were spilling all over. I could sit here all day, announcing the shift in the flakes and the fall.

And maybe, just maybe, I will . . .

A day of pure stillness is ours. And I intend to savor it all. And quiet my soul while I'm at it . . .

Insert (Joy) Here

Amid a long stretch of blur, amid headlines of "bloodbaths" at the newspaper that basically birthed the whole of this family, amid a national moment that left me wanting for a Lysol bath (in the infamous line my mother once uttered upon a trip home from a Las Vegas convention, the woes of the ad exec's dutiful wife), amid deadlines that have me typing from darkness to darkness, the tall bespectacled fellow with whom I reside (aka my lawful wedded husband) casually glanced out at the snows as I motored him off to yesterday's train. "It's my half-birthday today," he informed, as if that alone might be enough to save the day.

And it was, and it did, in its infinitesimal way.

The moment, which I latched onto, which I considered as I went about the eventual business of melting ice cream, hauling out a heart-shaped cookie cutter, as I sprinkled Ghirardelli chocolatey chips—plonk, plonk, plonk on the plate—sliced strawberries in quarters and halves, was not unlike a wisp of a comma in a long, long paragraph of words: easily missed, but emphatically necessary (ask any third-grade teacher of grammar).

The sense indecipherable without it.

Necessary, because in the seasons of life, some feel impossibly uphill; others, more feet-off-the-pedals, whiz-down-the-lane, hardly an effort at all. Necessary, because the human species is hard-wired for a break in the weather, a break in the onslaught. (I often wonder if that's why God invented seasons, and the turnings therein.) And sometimes we have to decidedly, deter-minedly, do that—engineer the breaks—all by ourselves. It's our job. We have to insert (joy) here. Insert (relief) there. Insert (closest thing to whimsy) precisely here.

My first wave of response, loosely holding the wheel, craning my neck to get a look at the half-birthday boy's face, was to utterly melt. To be charmed that the long-standing practice in this old house of making a fuss over fractional birthdays (as recently as noting someone's 26½) had rubbed off on the tall one. He'd never before in all these years mentioned his half birthday, though it comes a mere two days before the one we've been noting for the last 18 years. (Don't think I didn't try to mail half a birthday cake to faraway college...)

My second wave of response, the one that's stuck with me all day and over the night, is the not-so-big thought that sometimes it's up to us to take the reins of our joys, and our whimsies, and push away the worries, the angst, the unrelenting questions, for enough of a pause to let in a dribble of light.

Otherwise, we go dark. Endlessly dark.

And there's something particularly joyful about making your joys all by yourself. Home-spun joy. Joy barely noticed. Joy that comes from scrounging the pantry (too many deadlines to rush to the grocery). From reaching into the freezer and thinking ahead to melt the Tahitian-vanilla-bean ice cream (okay, so I had to take two passes at that part when I forgot I was in the middle of melting and found myself with a pint of oozy liquid vanilla). From reaching into the basket of heart-shaped cookie cutters, pulling out just the right one. From turning the lights out, striking a match, ferrying a heart + berries + chocolatey chips and flickering candle over to the half-birthday boy.

It was the tiniest wisp of a moment—surely a comma in a long string of words (try reading without that ink swirl on the page we know as the comma). But it ushered in an exclamation mark of momentary joy.

And that, at the midpoint of a year in the life of someone you love, is perfectly, positively necessary. And good.

Prayer for a
Still Winter's Morning

How did the heavens know? How did the Great Beyond know that I needed a morning's blanket?

I needed stillness to step into.

The night had been long, had been tumbled. It was one of those nights when worry stitches each one of your dreams. You awake, yes, but you wonder if you've slept even a wink.

All you need on a morning like that is softness. Is quiet. You need a world on its tiptoes, padded tiptoes. You need a morning that, like an old friend, understands without words. Sidles up beside you, lays its head on your shoulder. Breathes.

The morning comes softly. Snow tumbles down in flakes that shift from fat to fatter. You breathe. You inhale blessing, breath after breath, and then you let loose, your morning's litany, petition spiraling atop petition.

Dear God, watch over him. Dear God, protect her. Dear God, forgive us; forgive us our endless offenses, our trespasses, too. Dear God, forgive this globe that seems to be spinning too close to the edge of madness.

Dear God, fill us with grace. Give us strength. Give us wisdom. And, please, for once, let words fall from our lips with half the sense we'd hoped they would hold.

Dear God, blanket us. Open our eyes and our hearts. Show us the way. Let us startle someone in these hours ahead with some blast of unheralded goodness. Let us be the instrument of your peace. Let us pass over temptation, not be the one to whisper the word that would cut to the quick. Not turn the cold shoulder.

Dear God, steady us. Deepen us. Let me be the vessel this day that carries you into the midst of the chaos. Let me sow love. Let me bring pardon. Let me, in these hours ahead, scatter faith wherever there's doubt; hope, in place of despair.

You've answered my prayer before I've opened my eyes for the day. You've laced the dawn in white upon white, you've hushed the world out my window. You've opened my door into prayer—still heart, deep vow, bold promise.

Dear God, I thank you. Now let us tiptoe softly into this day.

Blessed Be February

The long dark weeks of winter wend, for Christians, deeper into Ordinary Time, until Lent begins, and with it the hope of purification, of burning away, cleansing, all that keeps us from holiness through and through. Depending how the calendar unfurls, Ash Wednesday often falls in middle to late February. It's in the fasting and abstinence of that hallowed day, when we're stained with the soot of burned bits of palm, that we embark on the forty-day journey into the uncharted terrain of the soul. In the words of poet and minister Jan Richardson, this is the Lenten call: "Let your heart break. Let it crack open. Let it fall apart so that you can see its secret chambers, the hidden spaces where you have hesitated to go." But don't stop there. "Let this be a season for wandering, for trusting the breaking, for tracing the rupture that will return you to the One who waits, who watches, who works within the rending to make your heart whole."

A Count-Your-Blessings Calendar

Fourteen Blessings for February

Here, fourteen blessings to wrap yourself in the end-of-winter's hardest won gifts—peace, quiet, and the contentment that feels most like purring. Especially when you're bursting to break out of February's days upon days of dreary.

Blessing 1: The earth's turning dollops one more minute of sunlight onto each February day. Ancient Celtic spirituality considered dawn and dusk especially permeable thresholds, "a time that is not a time," when the sacred is more apt to seep through. Consecrate the sacred hour. Tiptoe outdoors once twilight deepens into darkness. Read the night sky. When you spy a twinkling star, whisper a prayer of infinite thanks for heaven's lamplights.

Candlemas (Feb. 2): Amid the winter's darkness, pause to consider the blessing of the candles, ordained to illuminate the hours. Fill your kitchen table, gathering a flock of orphan candlesticks. Adorn with winter branches and berries clinging to the bough.

Blessing 3: Behold the hush of snowfall. The flakes free-falling past the porch light, their hard-angled intricacies and puffy contours tumbling, tumbling, lulling all the world and its weary citizens into that fugue state that comes with heavy snow—when at last we take in breath, and hold it. Fill our empty lungs.

Blessing 4: Be dazzled by the diamond-dusted world you just woke up to. The way the flakes catch bits of moonlight, shimmer like a thousand million stars. To be dazzled is a prayer.

Blessing 5: Sometimes winter pushes us to the ends of our hope. It can be the season of nearly giving up. But then the holy hallelujah comes—the red bird, the pure contentment of mere survival, the steaming bowl of soup when you come in from shoveling, winter's Sisyphean folly.

Blessing 6: Savor the sanctuary of being tucked in a cozy kitchen, looking out at a winter world of which we stand in awe. Bless the contemplative nature of this season that draws us into the depths of our cave, where we find fuel for the seasons still to come.

Valentine's Day (Feb. 14): Tuck love notes under pillows, inside lunch bags and coat pockets. Sprinkle a trail of construction-paper hearts from bedside to breakfast table, and christen the day with whimsies and joy. Murmur deep thanks for the gifts of heart.

Blessing 8: A radical thought about saints, in the wake of St. Valentine's feast day: We each, all of us, possess sparks of the Divine. Our holiest charge: Kindle the light. Touch one flame to another. Before it darkens. If we each spend one minute, one spark of the day, living beyond our small little selves, fairly soon we've ignited a bonfire.

Blessing 9: There are corners of the world, not far from our very front doors, where mercy is needed. Be merciful. Seek out the ones who have no one to turn to. Be the face of kindness, be kindness in the flesh.

Blessing 10: Words to carry you across a day without sunshine: "I am done with great things and big things, great institutions and big success, and I am for those tiny, invisible molecular moral forces that work from individual to individual, creeping through the crannies of the world like so many rootlets, or like the capillary oozing of water, yet which if you give them time, will rend the hardest monuments of man's pride." —William James, American philosopher and psychologist (1842-1910).

Blessing 11: Inscribe this instruction from that erudite preacher without a pulpit, Ralph Waldo Emerson, onto your heart: "The invariable mark of wisdom is to see the miraculous in the common." That means us, perched on a log in the woods. That means us, necks craned as we trace the shooting star.

Blessing 12: Some winters—some harsh and desolate winters inside our soul—we need surrender to the holy Earth, to the rhythms that sustain us, move us forward even when we don't believe we've the energy to lift a weary foot. Mother Earth comes to comfort us. She offers hope. Even when we cannot see it. Trust the invisible stirrings just beneath the surface.

Blessing 13: Back before the winter came, a last act of hope came the day we dropped to bent knee, thrust shovel in the ground, and tucked in dozens and dozens of bulbs. It's a form of prayer, is it not, to tuck hope beneath the earth, to step away, and await the moment when the surge comes, when the tender determined shoot of newborn green comes poking through the earth. Declares triumph. Offers proof that hope pays off.

Blessing 14: Bundle up for a meandering walk in the end-of-winter woods, marvel at the survival of so many species. Marvel at your own.

The February Kitchen:

By the time we flip the calendar page to February, some of us are careening toward stir-crazy, staring out the window laser-focused on spying the faintest glimmer of vernal hope. Perhaps the first tender nub, periscoping through earth's unyielding crust? How 'bout an extra warble of quarter notes woven into the cardinal's morning canticle? Nope. *Nada*. Zero. February is the fallow season. February is when we're thinking of calling it quits on all the stillness. What we need is full-throttle proof that something's stirring, underground *and* deep in our soul. The February kitchen offers a lifeline. Clang the pots, bang the pans. Haul out the double-necked beaters, or perhaps your bakery-grade mixer, the one that hijacks the counter. And thank heavens for the mid-month excuse to haul out the glitter, the glue, the laciest doilies, and drift upon drift of rosy-tinged frostings. It's the exuberant once-a-year license to whoop it up with an army of hearts. So many ways to say, "I love you." And break loose of the wintry ties that so bind.

Pause. Bow Head. Strike Sullen Pose.

"Did you see the obituaries?" my mother asked, first thing one October day in 2007. My mother was insistent, clearly undone. "Peg died."

Peg Bracken, she meant, iconic cookbook author and midcentury humorist who penned a monthly jab at domesticity in *Family Circle* magazine. Peg, who might as well have been our next-door neighbor growing up. The one who would have passed Virginia Slims over the picket fence. Poured a cocktail as soon as the kiddies polished off their after-school snack. I'm thinking her only use for her apron was to wipe her muddy shoes.

Despite—or because of—the anarchy, my mother consulted her. Followed her. Stood off in the corner of the kitchen with her, often, snickering in a most rebellious way.

She was, apparently, my mother's alter ego. She was, maybe, the trouble-maker my mother wasn't. She was, in 1960 when her cookbook came out—her anti-cookbook, really, *The I Hate to Cook Book*—a breath of something new in the simmering winds over by the range (for what had been the stove became the range somewhere in the latter half of the last century).

Her most famous recipe, perhaps, the one uncobwebbed for all the obits, is one called "Skid Road Stroganoff."

It goes like this:

"Start cooking those noodles, first dropping a bouillon cube into the noodle water. Brown the garlic, onion, and crumbled beef in the oil. Add the flour, salt, paprika, and mushrooms, stir, and let it cook five minutes while you light a cigarette and stare sullenly at the sink."

Even now, it's hard not to love a woman who whisks *sullenly* into a recipe for stroganoff.

In the house where I grew up, that blue book with the funny drawings—drawn, by the way, by Hilary Knight, who drew the daylights out of *Eloise at The Plaza*—stood mostly for one dish: a dish once named Chicken-Rice Roger. But in our house, now, it is mostly known as Chicken Rice Grammy, for it is the perfect embodiment of all things cozy in a covered dish.

It (a) comes bubbling out of the oven, (b) is made (unless you're a rule breaker) with stuff dumped from a can, and (c) is the surest cure for a bad day that I can think of.

And so, here's to Peg, now departed; Peg, who made my mother giggle. Peg, who had my mama dumping cans all around the kitchen. And to my mama, who's made this more Grammy Tuesdays than I could possibly count. And never sullenly.

Chicken Rice Grammy

When old-fashioned comfort food—nothing frilly or fancy or nouvelle about it—is the order of the day. When riffling through the banged-up recipe box unearths a morsel from your not-so-distant past, and a tucked-away era springs back to life as you go about your kitchen ministrations. When the whole point of dinner is simply to say, "I love you through and through."

Provenance: Peg Bracken's The I Hate to Cook Book
(I confess to a tad of tinkering here, as I've quashed dear Peg's tin-canned fixation.)

Yield: Serves 6, if not too hungry
- 4 to 6 chicken breasts, skinless and boneless, cut into halves
- ¾ cup uncooked rice (I opt for brown basmati rice)
- 1 cup mushrooms, sliced
- 1 onion, diced
- 1 ¾ cups chicken broth
- Salt and pepper, to taste
- Optional: ¾ cup artichoke hearts, red pepper strips, olives, whatever add-ins you fancy

1. Preheat oven to 350 degrees Fahrenheit. Grease a 9-inch baking dish. (I use a soufflé dish with lid.)

2. Brown chicken in sauté pan. Dump golden-browned chicken atop rice, mushrooms, onion, broth, and add-ins already placed in baking dish.

3. Bake, covered, for 1 hour. (If you're using brown rice, you might want to check at the half-hour mark and add a splash more chicken broth if needed.) As you disinter from the oven, tip your casserole lid to dear Peg, who despite her disinclination always delivered delicious.

Oma Lucille's Famous Rolled Cut-Out Cookie Hearts

In my growing-up days, the gravitational pull of any and every holiday drew us back to the familial roost, which meant a six-hour road trip, Chicago to Cincinnati, and my grandma's ivy-covered house on the hill. Once our old wood-paneled station wagon pulled to a stop at the bottom of the scary-steep driveway just outside the butter-bathed kitchen, we couldn't escape the wagon's confines quickly enough. We'd be in my grandma's ample arms, then slither past—swift as politely possible—headed straight to the tin of buttery cut-outs tucked belly-to-belly against the toaster. I've made these my go-to hearts ever since. For me, February's Festival of Hearts will forever signal the soundtrack of lifting the lid on a menagerie of hearts in a plethora of sizes and drizzles, all nesting atop crinkly wax-paper beds. As I look closely at the recipe card I pulled from my heirloom cookery file, I see a note that says this came from the kitchen of Elizabeth G., my grandpa's sister, Aunt Lily, yet another sturdy German baker, this one a Fräulein. Spinster sister, Aunt Lily was. Ah, but she begat these, and they live on, ever, they do . . .

Provenance: My Great-Aunt Lily, Elizabeth Glaser

Yield: Never enough

1 cup shortening
½ cup brown sugar
½ cup white sugar
1 egg
2 cups all-purpose flour
¼ teaspoon baking soda
¼ teaspoon salt
2 tablespoons lemon juice
1 teaspoon grated lemon rind (or one lemon, grated)
Cinnamon hearts, pressed into service as your whimsy
   desires

Lacy drizzle:
1 ½ cups confectioners' sugar
¼ teaspoon vanilla
5 to 6 teaspoons milk
2 to 3 drops food coloring gel

1. Cream shortening. Add sugars. Cream well, adding egg, flour, soda, salt, and, finally, lemon juice and rind.

2. Chill about 3 hours (or overnight).

3. Preheat oven to 350 degrees Fahrenheit. Roll to ¼-inch thickness.

4. Deploy cookie cutters. (Baker's note: As the season demands; here, we go with hearts, hearts, and more hearts, hearts the size of a saucer, hearts as itty-bitty as a postage stamp. And the rest of the year, roll out bunnies, chicks, or Easter eggs in spring; pumpkins, turkeys, Santa à la sleigh, as their occasions arise.)

5. Plunk cinnamon hearts where needed—or alternately, seasonally, try a raisin as bunny's nose, chick's beak, or, in time, Mr. Turkey's eye.

6. Bake 10 to 12 minutes, or until golden-rimmed.

7. Let cool on wire cooling rack. While your hearts are dozing, make your drizzle: Stir milk into confectioners' sugar, add vanilla; mix well. Drop in gel coloring, pink, red or otherwise (be sure to separate into individual bowls, one for each color). Drizzle to your heart's desire. Let sit till icing is firm to gentle touch.

8. Slide off cooling racks and settle onto wax-paper nests, or your prettiest platter or basket. Deliver to your sweetest sweethearts.

Uncle Bri's White Chili

One Christmas Eve so long ago I barely, fuzzily remember, I overeagerly decided to make a roster of chilies in a trio of Christmasy colors: one red, one white, *and* one green. The white handily rose to the top, and ever after it's my go-to wintry wake-up. Somehow, over the years, at least three white-chili variations crept into my much-splattered three-ring family-recipe binder. But after plenty of kitchen tinkering, I've distilled those three into this one. On a cold winter's night, it'll bring just the right zing to your table.

Provenance: Uncle Brian's yellowed, faded computer print-out, circa, 1990 + hand-scribbled notes from a long-forgotten source known, curiously, as the "Chili Heads." (Brian, for the record, is my beloved youngest brother.)

Yield: 8 bowls

> 2 pounds boneless, skinless chicken thighs (or breast meat, but thighs are tastier)
> 8 cups chicken stock
> 3 teaspoons oregano, crumbled (crumbling releases more flavor, simply pinch between fingers)
> ½ teaspoon marjoram

3 15-ounce cans white beans, drained (or 1 pound dry
   white beans*)
2 tablespoons extra-virgin olive oil
2 medium onions, chopped
4 cloves garlic, minced
4 teaspoons ground cumin
¼ teaspoon cayenne pepper
¼ teaspoon white pepper
¼ teaspoon ground cloves
1 4-ounce can chopped green chiles
1 red pepper, chopped
1 jalapeño or serrano pepper, finely chopped
   (optional)
¼ cup fresh cilantro, or as your heart desires
1 ½ cups grated Monterey Jack cheese

For serving: Put out bowls of Monterey Jack cheese,
   diced cilantro, diced peppers (red and/or jalapeño),
   black olive slices, sour cream, salsa, guacamole (pick
   and choose as you please)

*If cooking dry beans, add the following to water or stock:
3 teaspoons salt
2 cloves garlic
2 bay leaves

1. If using dry beans, cook them first: Place the beans in a medium pot and cover with a couple inches of hot water, about 2 quarts. (For even more flavor, cook in about 8 cups chicken stock, and when done use the bean broth for the chili, and even for poaching chicken.) Add salt to water, and add garlic and bay leaves to water or broth. Heat on high to bring to a simmer, cover, and reduce heat to very low to maintain a low simmer.

2. Cook for 2 to 3 hours or until the beans are cooked through and tender (note that cannellini beans will cook faster than navy beans, and older dry beans will take longer to cook than newer). Drain.

3. While beans are cooking, poach chicken in stock (I'm never shy about tossing herbs and spices—1½ teaspoons oregano and ½ teaspoon marjoram—into the stock; anything to dial up flavor). Cook till tender, about 15 minutes. Drain and cool. Using a fork or your fingers, shred the chicken into bite-size pieces. Set aside.

4. In a large thick-bottomed pot, sauté onions in olive oil on medium-high heat until tender, about 4 minutes. Add garlic, 1½ teaspoons dried oregano, cumin, cayenne and white pepper, and cloves, and cook a minute more. Add green chiles, and minced jalapeño or serrano pepper if using.

5. Add reserved, shredded, poached chicken and chicken stock back to the pot of onions and spices. Add drained cooked beans (or cans of beans) and simmer, stirring occasionally, about 1 to 1½ hours. Taste; add more salt and seasonings if needed. Depending

how salty your chicken stock and beans are, you may need to add a teaspoon or more.

Note: Like so many wintry soups, stews, and potages, chili only gets better when allowed to steep in its flavors. So feel free to cook a day or two ahead, and rest assured it will only deepen in deliciousness.

When it's time to chow down, ladle chili into bowls, and spread out a parade of chili fixings, each in its own bowl: grated cheese, diced cilantro, diced peppers (red and/or jalapeño), black olive slices, sour cream, salsa, and guacamole. Serve with fresh warmed flour tortillas, chips, or fat squares of corn bread.

Beef Stew Matters

A confession: for days now I've been considering the fine points of stew. I've pondered the layering of flavorful notes. Ruminated over anchovies. Weighed root vegetables. Detailed the pluses of rutabaga, countered with low points of turnip. I've dwelled on umami, that quixotic "fifth taste" we're all after.

At last, I've settled on a road map. Any hour now, I'll be cranking the flame, putting chunks of beef to iron-hot scald of my three-thousand-pound cook pot. It's what you do when you want a fine stew.

Because a wintry stew, served to a hungry tableau, is the *raison d'être* of the season of ice and blustery winds and bone-chilling temps that makes us ponder the wisdom of bears who pack it all up and go under cover from, say, the Thanksgiving feast till the rising of Easter.

I am filling my table with people I love, and a few whom I only scantily know. I am, after all, a believer in the power of putting ideas to the world, and the best place I know for birthing fine thought, for bridging frames of reference, is the dinner table. The way I see it, the dinner table is merely the classroom, the seminar chamber, set with knives, forks, and a battalion of glassware.

And, if you want to bring together great stews of ideas, of stories, of wisdom, of light, you need to stoke the flame with the richest, most sublime assemblage of feast and drink and, yes, a setting or two—or six—from the old-plate collection.

It's why I've been turning to my panel of master teachers, all lined up on the shelves of my kitchen—and a few who walk and talk and dispense real-life secrets. It's why I'm sidling up to David Tanis, a generous-hearted cook (formerly of Chez Panisse and a regular in the *New York Times*) endowed with a down-to-earth soul who finds perfection in a simple soft-boiled egg and who writes that the peeling of carrots and onions for a simple stew "can be meditative."

It's not about wow-ing. It's about allowing the feast to speak for the part of my heart and soul that breathes beyond words.

The equation I'm after is one that's infused with humility, yet banks on the notion that dolloping grace and delicious-ness—both in measures sublime—is bound to spiral the talk a notch or two and kindle the room with a shared sense of the sacred: this table matters, what unfolds here is sac-ramental; and, as the one who's done the gathering, I've infused it with the very best I could muster.

My Secret Ingredient Beef Stew

When a slow stir at the cookstove is the meditation you're after, and peeling and chopping and mashing entice, offering backbeat to your kitchen incantation. When you're hungry for take-it-up-a-notch feasting, and especially when there's a chill in the day, and you're out to blanket the ones you love with a bubbling pot that, more than anything, warms the soul.

Provenance: Ree Drummond, Pioneer Woman *blog + Amanda Hesser,* Food52 *blog + David Tanis, the* New York Times

Yield: 8 servings

2 tablespoons olive oil
3 pounds beef stew meat (chuck roast, cubed)
Salt and pepper, to taste
1 whole medium onion, diced
2 leeks, sliced
7 cloves garlic, minced
4 carrots, peeled and chopped
1 (8-ounce) package cremini (or baby bella)
    mushrooms

6 ounces tomato paste

2 anchovies, chopped

½-ounce packet dried porcini mushrooms*

½ cup red wine vinegar

1 cup canned whole tomatoes with juice

4 cups low-sodium beef broth, more if needed for thinning

1½ teaspoons salt

2 bay leaves

¾ teaspoon dried thyme

1 whole turnip, peeled and diced

½ rutabaga, peeled and diced

1 parsnip, peeled and diced

1 cup pearl onions (I use frozen)

⅓ cup fresh parsley, minced

* An optional splurge. Or if, like me, you've had a packet sitting on the pantry shelf for a rather long time and need a fine excuse to put it to work.

1. Pat stew meat dry, then salt and pepper it. Heat olive oil in a large, heavy pot over medium-high heat. Brown ⅓ of the stew meat until the outside gets nice and brown, about 2 minutes. (Turn it as it browns.) Remove the meat from the pot with a slotted spoon and put on a plate or in a bowl. Add the rest of the meat, in thirds, to the pot and brown it, too. Remove to the same plate or bowl; set aside.

2. Add the leeks, onion, and garlic to the pot, stirring to coat in all the brown bits at the bottom. Cook for 2 minutes, then add 2 carrots and cremini mushrooms and, again, cook for a few minutes. Add tomato paste and anchovies (secret ingredient number 1) to the pot. Stir it into the alliums and vegetables and cook for 2 more minutes.

3. Meanwhile, soak dried porcini mushrooms (secret ingredient number 2) in 1 cup warm water.

4. Add wine vinegar (secret ingredient number 3) and tomatoes with juice; break apart tomatoes with back of spoon. Pour in the beef broth, stirring constantly. Add salt, bay leaves, and thyme and bring to a boil. Stir in (drained and rough-chopped) porcini mushrooms; then add beef back to the pot, cover, and reduce the heat to low. Simmer, covered, for 1½ to 2 hours.

5. After 1½ to 2 hours, add 2 (or more) diced carrots, turnips, rutabaga, and parsnip to the pot. Stir to combine, put lid back on the pot, and let simmer for another 45 minutes to 1 hour. (Sauce should be thick, but if it seems too thick, splash in a bit of beef broth until it's to your liking.)

6. When root vegetables are tender, stir in half the minced parsley. Add salt and pepper to taste. Cool to room temperature. Retire to the fridge for a few hours or overnight. (This peaks deliciousness, I promise, though you could dive in now, hot off the stove, and be mighty delighted.)

7. Once it's chilled, skim off any fat from the surface. Reheat over low heat, letting the stew simmer 45 minutes to 1 hour before serving.

8. Serve piping hot with steamy mounds of mashed potatoes, letting the juice run amok. Just before serving, stir in half the remaining minced parsley and use the rest as garnish, sprinkled atop the stew. Sacramental, indeed.

Psst: Make-Ahead Mashers

File this under *Indispensable*. Proof that, every once in a rare while, life offers a run-around, a shortcut, a simplifier. And since there's nary a holiday—or Sunday night supper—that isn't improved by a heap of mashed taters, and since holidays seem to come with to-do lists two miles long, this proven instruction does double duty: 1.) it's melt-in-your-mouth delectable, and 2.) it becomes so a whole day—or two!—ahead of the oncoming traffic jam there in your kitchen. Fact is, there's little so comforting as tucking this marvel off in the fridge, knowing one extra something is crossed off your list. You might feel your shoulders sink softly into relax mode, minus one worry for the morrow. Put your feet up, crank the kettle, pour yourself a steamy mug of I-Got-This tea . . .

Provenance: Ree Drummond, Pioneer Woman *blog + Joel Robuchon*

Yield: Serves 10. Seriously.

    5 pounds russet or Yukon Gold potatoes
    ¾ cups butter, diced and kept well-chilled until used

1 (8-ounce) package cream cheese, softened
½ cup half-and-half
1 teaspoon salt or seasoned salt
1 teaspoon pepper

1. Cut unpeeled potatoes into same-size pieces, roughly 2-by-2-inches.
   Bring a large pot of water to a simmer, and add the potatoes.
   Bring to a boil and cook for 30 to 35 minutes. Fork should slide
   into potatoes with no resistance, and potatoes should almost, but
   not utterly, fall apart.

2. Drain potatoes in large colander. Once drained, place potatoes
   back into the dry pot and put the pot back on the stove. Over low
   heat, mash the potatoes, allowing all the steam to escape, before
   adding in other ingredients. (The late great Joel Robuchon,
   who has long held the most Michelin stars in the world, and thus
   qualifies as someone to whom we should have listened, claimed
   this "drying out" technique was the Number 1 Secret to what
   he called his "*pommes puree*," which is really just a fancy-pants
   way of saying "mashed taters." He opted for medium heat, and
   instructed to turn the potatoes vigorously with a spatula for 5
   minutes, to achieve *pommes* perfection.)

3. Now, turn off the stove. Add butter, cream cheese, and half-and-
   half. "Mash, mash, mash!" orders our Pioneer goddess. Next, add
   salt (or seasoned salt, or whatever salty blend on your shelf) and
   pepper, to taste.

4. Stir well and place in a medium-sized baking dish (butter the sides and bottom of the dish for easier excavation of mashed potatoes). Throw a few pats of butter onto the potatoes. If for some reason you're not opting for the make-ahead plan, forge on: place in a 350-degree oven and heat until butter is melted and potatoes are warmed through.

5. For those of you buying into the make-ahead plan (and, really, why wouldn't you?), don't touch the oven. Not yet, anyway. Instead, cover with foil your ready-to-go mashed potatoes, and retire them to the fridge for overnight slumber (or for as long as 2 days). When dinner's on the horizon, take your chilled vat of potatoes out of the fridge about 2 to 3 hours before serving time. Keep covered and bake in a 350-degree oven for about 20 to 30 minutes or until warmed through. I've been known, before tucking it all into the oven, to drizzle a wee bit more half-and-half, stirring gently into the mound, and, because I can't leave well enough alone, I sprinkle with paprika to brighten the palette. Lips will be licked, and that's a promise.

February

scarlet-feathered incandescence aflame against the white-on-white tableau . . .

pinecones crackling in the hearth . . .

mittens that dare to be lost, lest they're tethered to strings knotted and threaded through coat sleeves . . .

flour-dusted countertops on the afternoon my grandma's famed cut-out cookie hearts demand to be rolled and baked and sugary drizzled (see recipe, page 206) . . .

stacks of red + pink construction paper + squiggly-edged scissors = cutting to your heart's content a flock of paper hearts, laid out in a trail from the edge of the bed, clear to the kitchen table . . .

sliding into mud boots, traipsing the bedraggled garden, imagining—listening for—the stirrings below. . .

scribble your own here: